ZOE MINISTRIES INTERNATIONAL

HOW TO KNOW GOD'S VOICE
IN HIS PRESENCE

FACILITATOR MANUAL

Copyright © 1998, 2023
All rights reserved.

This manual or parts thereof may not be reproduced, stored or transmitted in any form by any means without prior written permission of ZOE Ministries International, except as provided by United States of America copyright law.

ZOE Ministries International
P.O. Box 2207
Arvada, CO 80001 USA
permissions@zoemin.org

All scripture quotations, unless otherwise indicated, are taken from the *Holy Bible, New International Version* ® NIV ® Copyright © 1973, 1978, 1984 by Biblica, Inc. ® Used by permission of Zondervan. All rights reserved worldwide. www.zondervan.com.

Some quotes taken from *The NIV Study Bible*. Copyright © 1985 by The Zondervan Corporation Used by permission of Zondervan Publishing House.

Scripture quotations are taken from the *The Message*. Copyright © 1993 by Eugene H. Peterson. Used by permission of NavPress Publishing Group.

Scripture quotations marked (AMP) are taken from *The Amplified Bible, Old Testament*. Copyright © 1965, 1987 by The Zondervan Corporation. *The Amplified New Testament*, copyright © 1954, 1959, 1987 by the Lockman Foundation. Used by permission.

Quotes used by permission from Finis Jennings Dake, Sr., Author of *Dake's Annotated Reference Bible*.

Some quotes taken from *Daily Bible Study—Gospel of John*. Copyright © 1976 William Barclay. Used by permission of Westminster John Knox Press and Hymns-Ancient & Modern.

Some quotes taken from *Daily Bible Study—Gospel of Mark*. Copyright © 1976 William Barclay. Used by permission of Westminster John Knox Press and Hymns-Ancient & Modern.

Some quotes taken from *Daily Bible Study—Gospel of Luke*. Copyright © 1976 William Barclay. Used by permission of Westminster John Knox Press and Hymns-Ancient & Modern.

Thayer's Greek-English Lexicon of the New Testament by Joseph H. Thayer, copyright 2000 by Hendrickson Publishers, Peabody, Massachusetts. Used by permission. All rights reserved.

Some quotes taken from the *New International Dictionary of New Testament Theology, Vol. 2*. Copyright © 1967, 1969, 1971 by Theologisher Verlag Rolf Brockhaus, Wuppertal. Used by permission of Zondervan Publishing House.

Quote taken from *The International Bible Commentary* by F.F. Bruce. Copyright © 1986 Marshall, Morgan & Scott. Use by permission of Zondervan Publishing House.

Quote from Judson Cornwall's *Let Us Worship* used with permission from Bridge-Logos Publishers.

Quote from *Worship, The Missing Jewel* by A.W. Towzer (Camp Hill, PA: Christian Publications, Inc., 1992) reprinted with permission.

Quotations from the *FireBible®: English Standard Version* used by permission of Life Publishers International, 1625 N Robberson Ave, Springfield, MO 85803 U.S.A., www.lifepublishers.org.

Rev. 2/23

ACKNOWLEDGMENTS

ZOE Ministries International is dedicated to equipping, training and sending believers into all the world to minister by the leading of the Holy Spirit. This ministry helps build the body of Christ and encourages God's people to use their gifts and talents for His glory. It is for this purpose that this manual has been compiled by the leading of the Holy Spirit and the input of many people. ZOE Ministries wishes to thank them for their support, time, and talents in putting this manual together. We give our Lord all the **praise** and **glory** for this work!

CONTENTS

Foreword		...7
Introductory Comments to Facilitators		...9
Lesson 1	Introduction	...11
Lesson 2	Being Loosed!	...31
Lesson 3	Untie the Colt—The Lord Has Need of it!	...53
Lesson 4	Jesus, Our Passover Lamb	...67
Lesson 5	Betrayal versus Love	...85
Lesson 6	Decisions—Stage One	...103
Lesson 7	Humiliation—Stage Two	...125
Lesson 8	Our Choice—Stages Three and Four	...141
Lesson 9	The Robe, the Crown and the Cross—Stages Five and Six	...157
Lesson 10	Carrying the Cross—Stages Seven and Eight	...167
Lesson 11	Departure From His Presence—Stages Nine and Ten	...183
Lesson 12	Past the Veil and Into His Presence	...197
Endnotes		...213
Appendix		...221

This material is designed to be used within a specific format. Facilitator Training is a necessary prerequisite before this material may be used effectively in a Bible study or class setting.

ZOE MINISTRIES INTERNATIONAL

FOREWORD

Dear Facilitator,

In **Revelation 2:4** Jesus speaks to the church at Ephesus, telling them that they have forsaken their first love for Him. How easy it is to allow the cares of the world to slip into our lives and replace that "first love" we had when we first accepted Jesus as our Lord.

This course, *In His Presence*, brings us once again to the cross and the significant part it plays in our lives. We take an intense look at the last week of Jesus' life, examining how He laid down His life so that we might have eternal life.

Like all the courses in ZOE's "Knowing" series, this course causes us to fall deeper in love with our Lord Jesus. It is His desire that daily we walk in close communion with Him, and that we are familiar with not only His deeds, but His ways as well.

This is truly a soul-searching course designed for people who have an understanding of the character of God and His love for us. We know that this course will change your life—as it truly impacted ours! We pray that the Holy Spirit will refresh and renew a deep love for Jesus in your heart and in the hearts of all the class members.

Enjoy!

Dick and Ginny Chanda
Founding Directors

INTRODUCTORY COMMENTS
TO FACILITATORS

As an introduction to this manual, we have summarized information that we feel will be helpful to you during this course. Most of this information was covered during your facilitator training.

- DIRECTIONAL INFORMATION FOR FACILITATORS IS OUTLINED IN THIS FONT FOR QUICK IDENTIFICATION.

- Remember, do not just teach this material unless you are instructed to do so in the manual. As a facilitator, you need to remember that you are a coach and are there to encourage class participation.

- The first few lessons will have a more instructional format. Some of the early lessons include teachings that provide a common base of understanding for your class members.

- If a lesson contains a teaching, please let the class know that you are teaching from the Facilitator Manual provided by ZOE Ministries International.

- **In this course you will lead all the Scripture discussions. Model leading the book and article discussions in Lessons 1–3. Participants will lead the book and article discussions beginning in Lesson 4. Tell the class that all should prepare to lead these discussions each week and that you will ask one of them to lead the discussions once you are together in class.**

- **As lead facilitator, you should have a copy of Max Lucado's book** *No Wonder They Call Him The Savior.* **In some lessons, the** *Facilitator Manual* **will prompt you to read aloud an excerpt from it in class.**

- As a facilitator, it is your responsibility to encourage the class to share the insights God gave them as they studied the assigned material. Ask questions that will draw out these insights.

- You are not expected, nor should you attempt, to cover every point in each lesson, especially if you have less than 2 1/2 hours of class time. These points are provided for your edification and those that directly support the main principle should be included in the class discussion.

- As participants become more involved in leading class discussions, your primary purpose is to coordinate the class and allow the Lord to build individuals' confidence and leadership abilities.

- During a class discussion, if someone's answer or insight is not scripturally correct or not related to the discussion, please do not directly address this with the individual. Instead, redirect the discussion back to the main principle of the lesson.

- Remember, as a facilitator, you cannot solve each person's problems. You are to present principles from God's Word and allow the Holy Spirit to help class members apply them to their lives.

- Finally, we respectfully ask that this copyrighted material not be copied or reproduced for other purposes without express written permission from ZOE Ministries International. We request this not to "control" the material, but for two reasons: 1) Without proper facilitator training, the course will not be what we feel the Holy Spirit wants it to be, and 2) We need to honor those who have graciously given us permission to reprint or quote their materials. As stewards of their authorship, we are responsible for not using this material beyond the limitations that they have requested.

Thank you for your involvement in this ZOE course and we join you in praying that the Holy Spirit will transform participants' lives!

IN HIS PRESENCE

LESSON 1

INTRODUCTION—MAN'S FALL AND SEPARATION FROM GOD

MAIN PRINCIPLE

Mankind has been separated from God because of our sin, but from the beginning God made provision to restore the fellowship He so desires to have with us. It is through Jesus' sacrifice and shedding of His blood that we can be in right standing with God, enter into God's presence with confidence, and have fellowship with Him.

LESSON 1

Introduction

I. **Let's Get Started!**

   A. WELCOME THE CLASS.

   B. OPEN WITH PRAYER.

   C. GET ACQUAINTED BY ASKING PARTICIPANTS TO BRIEFLY SHARE SOMETHING ABOUT THEMSELVES, E.G., WHETHER THEY ARE MARRIED, HAVE CHILDREN, ETC. BEGIN BY SHARING ABOUT YOURSELF.

   D. HAVE SOMEONE READ THE MAIN PRINCIPLE FOR THIS LESSON.

   NOTE: A TIME OF WORSHIP IS SUGGESTED IN SECTION IV, AFTER REVIEWING THE PARTICIPANTS' RESPONSIBILITIES.

II. **Introduction to ZOE Ministries International**

   NORMALLY THIS COURSE IS LIMITED TO THOSE WHO HAVE ALREADY TAKEN OTHER ZOE COURSES, SO PARTICIPANTS ARE ALREADY FAMILIAR WITH ZOE MINISTRIES INTERNATIONAL. HOWEVER, IF AN EXCEPTION HAS BEEN MADE AND SOMEONE NEW TO ZOE IS IN YOUR CLASS, TAKE THIS PARTICIPANT ASIDE AFTER CLASS AND REVIEW A VISION CARD OR LESSON 1 OF THE HEARING GOD'S VOICE MANUAL.

III. Overview of This 12-Week Course

A. The Purpose of This Course

1. To come out of the doldrums in our relationship with Jesus

2. To have an intimate, vibrant and refreshing relationship with Him

3. To enable us to enter more fully into the presence of our Father

4. To fall in love again with Jesus and with the Father by the power of the Holy Spirit

B. How Will We Accomplish This?

1. By looking afresh at the last week of Jesus' life

2. By examining our hearts and our motives

3. By imitating Jesus and His obedience to the Father

4. By looking at Jesus' times of suffering and victory

C. Class Materials

1. The Study Guide—includes a course outline, which gives the Scripture and the book assignment for each week, as well as supporting articles.

2. A Bible—Any acceptable translation. There will be a Scripture assignment each week. You will need to read and meditate on this Scripture at home. Ask the Holy Spirit to teach you as you study and take notes.

3. *Holiness, Truth and the Presence of God* by Francis Frangipane will be used as a textbook in this course. Each week there will be a reading assignment of a few chapters to be read at home.

D. Class Format of Lessons 2–12

1. Each class begins with 20–30 minutes of worship (10–15 minutes for a 1 1/2 hour class) unless in a shortened class.

2. 20–30 minutes (15–20 minutes) will be spent discussing the book assignment. Everyone comes prepared to share what they learned from the reading during the week.

3. We will spend 35–45 minutes (30 minutes) on the Scripture discussion. Everyone is encouraged to share the insights that God gave them as they studied the assigned Scriptures.

4. 15 minutes (10 minutes) will be spent discussing the assigned articles.

5. A prayer and ministry time is not necessary for every lesson. There will be times when the material is very impacting, as we realize more fully what Jesus did on the cross, and someone may need to receive ministry. There will be times when a period of silence will follow the discussions.

6. The facilitator will end each class with a closing prayer.

Lesson 1 — Introduction

E. Participant's Responsibilities

1. You will be expected to read the assigned Scriptures, the book chapters and articles each week and be ready to share the insights God gave you during the week. Come willing to share how God is asking you to apply these principles in your life, as the Spirit leads.

   This is a very exciting time as the Holy Spirit renews your relationship with Jesus and shows you how to come into God's presence more fully.

2. This course is a bit different from the typical ZOE course. Because of the sensitive nature of the material in this course, the facilitator leads each Scripture discussion.

3. Participants may be asked to lead the book or article discussions. The facilitator may ask someone to lead one of those discussions, depending on how the Holy Spirit leads. *So, everyone needs to come prepared to lead the book and article discussions each week.*

4. Keeping a daily journal is *strongly suggested*. It is very helpful to record your experience of how the reading impacted your life during the week preceding each class. Bring your journal to class to aid you in sharing the Scriptures, insights, direction, prayers and answers to prayer that the Lord gives you.

   For guidelines on maintaining a journal, read the handout on journaling found in the front section of your Study Guide.

5. Spend time with God *daily*. The Lord does not show favoritism—what He has done for others, He will do for you! Avoid last minute studying. Growth will come as you respond to God's Holy Spirit in your daily life.

6. In addition, please keep confidential everything that is shared during class.

IV. Worship the Lord

ALLOW ABOUT 20–30 MINUTES (10–15 MINUTES FOR A 1 1/2 HOUR CLASS).

V. Lesson 1 Teaching

A. Introduction

1. In this course we want to renew our love relationship with Jesus. In Revelation 2:4–5 Jesus speaks to the church at Ephesus: "Yet I hold this against you: You have forsaken your first love. Remember the height from which you have fallen! Repent and do the things you did at first."

    This Scripture points out that when we were first born again, when we first realized what Jesus did for us, our love for Him was vibrant. When we first loved Jesus it was as if we were on a mountaintop. How easy it is to fall down from that height!

2. Many of us tend to get involved in Christian works rather than pursue an intimate relationship with Christ. Many of us begin to look to God only for what He can do for us. We forget to ask what God

wants. It doesn't occur to us to seek His face, asking what is on His heart and mind.

During this course God wants us to seek His face,
not His hand.

---

3. God wants us to develop our relationship with Him. God wants us to better understand what Jesus Christ did for us—that He came to earth and offered Himself as a sacrificial lamb so that we might enter into a closer relationship with our wonderful, holy Father.

    But before we examine what Jesus has done for us, we must first look back at Genesis to see what God created and what type of relationship God desired to have with mankind.

4. READ THE ARTICLE "BETWEEN HEAVEN AND EARTH." HAVE PARTICIPANTS TAKE TURNS READING PORTIONS ALOUD. SAY THAT PARTICIPANTS MAY PASS IF THEY DON'T FEEL COMFORTABLE READING ALOUD. FACILITATE A BRIEF DISCUSSION, ASKING QUESTIONS TO DRAW OUT COMMENTS ABOUT THIS ARTICLE.

B. God's Perfect Relationship with Man

READ **GENESIS 1:26-31**.

1. Verse 26 says, "Then God said, 'Let us make man in our image, in our likeness.'"

Man in verse 26 is translated from the Hebrew word `adam (aw-dawm´), which means mankind or human being and includes both male and female.[1]

2. Both man and woman were a special creation of God, created in the *image* and *likeness* of God.

//

On the basis of this likeness, they could respond to
and have fellowship with God and uniquely reflect
His love, glory and holiness.

//

3. They were intended to reflect God's character as they exercised dominion over all the earth (**verse 26**).

4. They possessed a moral likeness to God, for they were sinless and holy, possessing wisdom, a heart of love and the will to do right. In **Ephesians 4:24** it says that we are **"created to be like God in true righteousness and holiness."**

5. What a relationship they must have had! **Psalm 8:3–9** gives a sense of what it was like. HAVE THE CLASS READ THESE VERSES. God entrusted to them dominion over all the earth.

6. Mankind lived with God in a personal fellowship that involved moral obedience and intimate communion.

C. Man Goofed—Not God!

1. READ **GENESIS 2:8–9**.

a. Humankind was placed in a perfect setting. It was a lavish, enjoyable garden, which included trees and a river (**verses 9–10**).

b. God made all kinds of trees **"that were pleasing to the eye and good for food" verse 9**. Among the trees in the garden was one tree that produced life and another that produced knowledge. These two trees were located in the middle of the garden, apparently close to each other. They provided the basis upon which Adam and Eve's obedience would be tested.

2. READ **GENESIS 2:15–17**.

    a. In **verse 15** it says that God put man in the garden **"to work it and take care of it."** The word *work* is translated from the Hebrew word *abad* (aw-bad´), which can mean to serve.[2] Consequently, the work that man did in the garden could, therefore, be described as his service to God.

    b. In **verse 16** we read of God's first command to mankind. It concerned life and death, good and evil. As with many of God's commandments, this command gave permission to do something positive along with a prohibition against doing something negative.

    c. God's command was given to Adam as a moral test. It placed before him a conscious, deliberate choice to believe and obey or to disbelieve and disobey his Creator's will.

d. Adam and Eve were created human beings, possessing a spirit and a soul—a mind, emotions and the power of choice.

e. God gave them permission to eat the fruit from any tree except the tree of the knowledge of good and evil. They could have chosen to eat from the tree of life.

   The word *life* here is translated from the Hebrew word *chay* (khah´-ee), which means remaining alive, flourishing, reviving, having immortality.[3]

f. **Verse 17** makes it clear that choosing to eat from the tree of the knowledge of good and evil would bring death.

g. As long as they believed what God said and obeyed, they would continue in eternal life and in blessed fellowship with God. If they sinned by disobeying, they would reap moral disaster and a harvest of death. READ **DEUTERONOMY 30:14-20.**

h. When Adam and Eve sinned, their moral likeness to God was marred.

3. READ **GENESIS 3:1–11.**

   a. In **verse 3** Eve referred to what God had said in **Genesis 2:17: "…When you eat of it you will surely die."** When they made the choice to sin, spiritual death occurred immediately, while physical death came later.

Lesson 1 — Introduction

    b. God's spiritual life in Adam and Eve died, and their human natures were corrupted. This spiritual death meant that their former relationship with God was destroyed.

    c. In **verse 7** Adam and Eve tried to cover themselves with fig leaves. In **verses 8–10** Adam and Eve hid when they heard God calling them.

///

Sin just as surely separates us from God. It harms our relationship with God, causing us to want to cover our sin and avoid God.

///

    d. The following quote comes from H.A. Maxwell Whyte's book *The Power of the Blood:*

> Right at the beginning of creation, God commanded that living creatures, greatly beloved of Adam, must be slaughtered by him and their blood must be shed to supply a covering for Adam and Eve's obvious nakedness. Fig leaves were insufficient. So animals were slaughtered and after the blood was shed, Adam and Eve were covered with the skins. The principle of a life for a life runs throughout the Bible. No other garments would sufficiently cover Adam and Eve except those which involved the shedding of blood. If man is left to himself he usually invents religions that do not require the shedding of blood. These are fig leaf religions.[4]

e. Adam and Eve felt afraid and were uncomfortable in God's presence. In this condition, they found it impossible to confidently draw near to Him.

4. READ **GENESIS 6:5–6**.

   a. Following man's fall, we never really see repentance.

   b. By this time, mankind had fallen to an all-time low. Man's depravity was described aptly in verse 5: "…every inclination of the thoughts of his heart was only evil all the time."

   c. Mankind's relationship with God was also at an all-time low.

D. The Father Seeks Relationship

1. READ ALOUD THE ARTICLE "THE BOY WITH THE SHINING FACE."

2. READ **GENESIS 12:1–3**.

   a. These verses describe God's call of Abraham. This call began a new direction in the Old Testament in which God revealed His purpose to redeem and save humanity. God's plan was to find a person who would know and serve Him with devoted faith, a person who would willingly fellowship with Him.

   b. From this man, Abraham, would come a family who would know, keep and teach the ways of the Lord. From this family would come a chosen nation of people who would be separated from the ungodly ways of other nations and who would do God's will. From this nation would come Jesus Christ.

3. READ **EXODUS 19:4–13**.

   a. In **verse 8** the people said, **"We will do everything the Lord has said."**

   b. In **verse 10** God told Moses to gather the people of the nation of Israel and consecrate them. Moses told them to wash their clothes and be ready to meet with God by the third day.

A cleansing needs to take place before entering the presence of the Lord.

---

   c. In **verse 11** God promised that the Israelites would see God's visible presence, but there were limits beyond which they could not pass. They could approach the mountain, but they could not ascend it (**verses 12–13**).

   d. One might ask, "Why this limit?" It was because God knew their hearts. The later reactions of the people (**Exodus 20:18–21**) clearly demonstrated that they were not qualified—nor did they truly desire—to enter into closer relationship with God.

   e. Despite what the people said in **verse 8** ("We will do everything the Lord has said"), the nation of Israel rejected a trusting, obedient type of relationship with God.

How To Know God's Voice—In His Presence

There are conditions that must be met in order to receive a fresh revelation of God.

4. READ **EXODUS 24:1–11**.

   a. In **verses 1–2** God invited a select group of men from the nation of Israel to come and worship Him—Moses, Aaron, Nadab, Abihu and 70 elders. Notice that the size of the group God was calling into relationship with Him was decreasing.

   b. These elders were called to worship, indicating a more intimate relationship with the Lord than the nation of Israel enjoyed as a whole.

   c. In **verses 4–8** we see the shedding of blood for the sins of the people. Again, we see that cleansing is necessary before entering God's presence.

   d. These men experienced an extraordinary revelation of God! **Verse 11** says that they saw God and ate and drank with Him.

   The word *saw* is translated from the Hebrew word *chazah* (khaw-zaw´), which means to see or behold. This word is used of the actual sight of the divine presence.[5] They must have experienced God's presence in a very real and conscious way.

   e. Their experience of God was far beyond that of the rest of the Israelites, but it effected no permanent transformation. Only a short time

Lesson 1 — Introduction

later they were found worshiping the golden calf (**Exodus 32**).

They were permitted to see God, but their subsequent behavior showed that they were not qualified to ascend to the top of the mountain into deeper fellowship with God.

    f. It becomes clear to us that mankind needed God's intervention to restore fellowship with Him.

E. God's Provision for Restored Fellowship

1. READ **GENESIS 3:15**.

    a. This verse contains the first promise of God's plan for redemption of the world. It prophesied a spiritual conflict between the offspring of the woman—Jesus Christ—and the offspring of the serpent—Satan and his followers. It predicts the ultimate victory of God and humankind over Satan and evil.

God provided a way for us to cleanse our guilty consciences, free us from sin, and restore us to fellowship with Him— through Jesus Christ.

---

    b. The redemption God provided through his Son allows us to draw near to God in order to receive His love, mercy, grace and help in times of need.

2. **Isaiah 53** prophesied about Jesus, God's suffering Servant.

a. **Isaiah 53:5** says, **"The punishment that brought us peace was upon him."** We sinful humans can have peace and reconciliation with our holy God because Jesus paid the penalty for our sins.

b. **Isaiah 53:11** also prophesied about Jesus. In *The Amplified Bible* it reads as follows:

> **He shall see [the fruit] of the travail of His soul and be satisfied; by His knowledge of Himself [which He possesses and imparts to others] shall My [uncompromisingly] righteous One, My Servant, justify many and make many righteous (upright and in right standing with God), for He shall bear their iniquities and their guilt [with the consequences, says the Lord].**

> **It is through Jesus' suffering and shedding of His blood that we can be in right standing with God and confidently enter into His presence. Through Jesus, we can fellowship with the Father and come to know Him more intimately.**

3. READ **JOHN 3:16-18**.

The key phrase in this passage is **"for God so loved."** God's desire for relationship was so great that He chose to send His one and only Son to earth, to offer Himself as a sacrificial lamb. Through His sacrifice, we may once again enter into the fullness of relationship with God.

It is amazing that the Father would love us so deeply that He would do this for us. Furthermore, it is just as amazing that Jesus, out of His faithful obedience, love for His Father and great passion for you and me, would willingly offer Himself in this way. It is too awesome for us to fully comprehend with our finite minds.

"For God so loved..." If only we could more fully understand the passionate love of the Father and the Son by the help of the precious, wonderful Holy Spirit! It is this love that bids us enter into God's presence.

F. Conclusion

Wonderful things are promised to those who choose to do what is needed to come into the presence of God.

1. READ **ISAIAH 4:2–6**. This passage prophesies about the people who will survive the coming judgment. They **"will be called holy"** and they will have the character of God, who is **"the Holy One of Israel" Isaiah 1:4**.

   In other words, they will be separated from the sinful world, cleansed by Christ's blood from all defilement, and regenerated by the Holy Spirit. Over them the glory of God will hover like a canopy (**verse 5**).

2. In **Psalm 16:11** the psalmist writes, **"You have made known to me the path of life; you will fill me with joy in your presence, with eternal pleasures at your right hand."**

God will show us the path that brings life. We will experience great joy when we come into God's presence. We are promised pleasures that will extend into eternity.

VI. Discussion of Class Articles

HAVE PARTICIPANTS TAKE TURNS READING PORTIONS ALOUD. FACILITATE A BRIEF DISCUSSION, ASKING QUESTIONS TO DRAW OUT COMMENTS ABOUT EACH ARTICLE. READ AND DISCUSS LAST THE ARTICLE **"THE RIVER OF GOD'S PLEASURE."**

VII. Next Week's Assignment

A. REVIEW THE ASSIGNMENT FOR LESSON 2 ON THE COURSE OUTLINE.

B. REVIEW THE MAIN PRINCIPLE FOR NEXT WEEK'S LESSON. ASK THE CLASS TO KEEP THE MAIN PRINCIPLE IN MIND AS THEY DO THE READING.

VIII. Today's Prayer and Ministry Time

A. A MINISTRY TIME WILL **NOT** ORDINARILY BE INCLUDED IN EACH WEEK'S LESSON.

  1. HOWEVER, IF YOU SENSE THE LORD DIRECTING YOU TO MINISTER TO SOMEONE, ASK THE PERSON CONCERNED IF HE/SHE WOULD LIKE PRAYER.

  2. AS FACILITATOR, YOU NEED TO GUIDE THE MINISTRY TIME. REFER TO THE

"CLASS FORMAT" SECTION OF THE *FACILITATOR TRAINING STUDY GUIDE* AND READ THE SECTION "MINISTRY TIME" AS NEEDED. (Note: *The Facilitator Training Study Guide* is the book you received during Facilitator Training.)

B. END THE LESSON BY PRAYING A CLOSING PRAYER. BE SENSITIVE TO THE HOLY SPIRIT'S GUIDANCE REGARDING HOW TO PRAY. YOU MIGHT WANT TO PRAY WITH THE MAIN PRINCIPLE IN MIND. A SAMPLE PRAYER FOLLOWS:

Dear Lord, thank You for wanting to fellowship with each of us. Thank You for wanting us to come into Your presence. Thank You, Jesus, for shedding Your blood for us so that we can come to the Father with confidence. Over the next twelve weeks, help us to come into Your presence more fully and more often. We pray in Jesus' precious name, Amen.

IN HIS PRESENCE

LESSON 2

BEING LOOSED!

MAIN PRINCIPLE

If we are in any kind of bondage, our understanding of the principles laid down for us by Jesus may be hindered. We need to ask the Holy Spirit to begin to unwrap for us any areas in which we are bound.

WWW.ZOEMINISTRIES.ORG

LESSON 2

Being Loosed!

I. Let's Get Started!

   A. WELCOME THE CLASS AND ENCOURAGE PARTICIPANTS TO SHARE WHAT GOD HAS DONE IN THEIR LIVES THIS PAST WEEK.

   B. OPEN WITH PRAYER.

   C. WORSHIP THE LORD.

   D. HAVE SOMEONE READ THE MAIN PRINCIPLE FOR THIS LESSON.

II. Review

   A. Last week we learned about the fall of mankind and how sin brought spiritual death to Adam and Eve. We learned that sin in our lives disrupts our fellowship with our holy God.

   B. We read Scriptures promising that the Messiah would provide us with righteousness, right standing with God. In **Genesis 3:15**, God promised to send the offspring of the woman—Jesus—to destroy the serpent's (Satan's) offspring. John had this passage in mind when he wrote that the Son of God came to destroy the devil's work in **1 John 3:8**.

   C. What is meant by **"the devil's work"**? Adam and Eve got a taste of it when the serpent tempted them to sin, which brought about death. In **John 10:10** Jesus said, **"The thief [Satan] comes only to steal and kill and destroy; I have come that they may have life, and have it to the full."** God's intention from the beginning was for us to have abundant life. Through His death, Jesus has restored the possibility of abundant life for us.

III. Supporting Principles From Scripture— John 11

A. Introduction

1. **Romans 5:12 says, "Therefore, just as sin entered the world through one man, and death through sin, and in this way death came to all men, because all sinned."** Sin's horrible consequence was death. Physical death can serve as an illustration of sin's effect in the spiritual realm. As physical death ends life and separates people, so sin causes separation of people from God and the life that is in God.

2. Just as Adam lost access to the fullness of God's life, those who reject Jesus will also lose that fullness of life. God made complete provision for abundant life through Jesus alone; there is no other way.

3. Raising Lazarus from the dead was the climactic miracle by which Jesus publicly provided evidence of His true claim: **"I am the resurrection and the life."**

4. Jesus had been preaching in the villages beyond the Jordan before He received news of Lazarus' sickness (**John 11:3**).

5. This third miracle of resurrection was the most remarkable of all Jesus' mighty works. It occurred one month before Jesus was crucified, and it foreshadowed His own death and resurrection.

B. John 11:1–3

1. As Mary and Martha's brother grew very sick, the sisters turned to Jesus for help. They believed in His ability to help because they had seen His miracles. They both felt that disease would flee at Jesus' presence.

We can call out to Jesus for healing of sin or sickness that has invaded our lives.

---

2. They did not describe the type of sickness or give details. It was serious enough for the sisters to request the aid of their Healer Friend, who loved them.

3. They were sure that Jesus would respond because of His love for Lazarus. They did not say, **"Come."** They just said, **"Lord, the one you love is sick."** They believed this would not fail to bring Him to them.

    The word *love* in this phrase is translated from the Greek word *phileo* (fil-eh´-o), which means **"to be a friend to, to have affection for, denoting personal attachment...."**[1]

4. It is interesting that they said, "the one you love," not "the one who loves you, Jesus." D.L. Moody once said, "I am greatly impressed when I hear someone sharing how much he loves God, but I am deeply touched when I hear someone share about how much the Lord loves him."[2]

Our love for God is hardly worth mentioning, but His love for us can never be proclaimed enough.

When we can speak of God's love for us, we have begun to experience walking in His presence.

C. **John 11:4**

1. But Jesus did not go to Lazarus immediately. His delay was not motivated by lack of love or by fear of His persecutors. Jesus waited until the right moment in order to fulfill the Father's plan.

2. In **verse 4** Jesus said, **"This sickness will not end in death. No, it is for God's glory so that God's Son may be glorified through it."** This was the message most likely sent back to the two sisters.

3. When Jesus received the sisters' message, He already knew the facts of the situation. How do you think Jesus knew about Lazarus' sickness?

4. He said to the messenger and to His disciples that such a sickness would not end in death. But God permitted a temporary death for two reasons, 1) to fulfill the glory of God, and 2) to glorify Jesus Himself.

5. Lazarus must have died shortly after the message was sent. Jesus was about 18 miles away. It took one day for the messenger to reach Jesus; then Jesus waited two days, and it took an additional day for Jesus to walk to Bethany.

D. John 11:5–6

1. Let's look at these three people Jesus loved. Martha, Mary and Lazarus were all very different. It is apparent that Jesus loves various personalities.

    a. He loved Martha—the active, practical keeper of the home, intent on assuring the comfort of her guests (**Luke 10:38–40**).

    b. He loved Mary—the contemplative, spiritual woman of insight and tender sympathy.

    c. He loved Lazarus—a man of few words, quiet and unobtrusive. We don't read much about Lazarus, but the name Lazarus means **"God helpeth."**[3] This miracle certainly confirmed that God was Lazarus' help!

2. Jesus dealt with each according to his or her individual gifts or inclinations, as is mentioned in **Proverbs 22:6: "Train up a child in the way he should go [and in keeping with his individual gift or bent], and when he is old he will not depart from it" (AMP).**

    a. To Martha, Jesus was eternal life. To Mary, He was incarnate love. To Lazarus, Jesus was the mighty Lord. Who is Jesus to you?

b. He knows us individually (**Psalm 139**). He deals with us according to our individual gifts and bents. What He is doing in one person's life is different from what He is doing in another's.

3. We don't know how often Jesus visited the home of Mary, Martha and Lazarus. However, it seems that this home in Bethany was a place of refuge for Jesus (**Matthew 21:17; Mark 11:11; Luke 10:38**). Jesus loved this family. He did not neglect this love; He waited for the appropriate time to demonstrate greater love and power to them.

4. D.L. Moody said, "Love must be active, as light must shine. As someone has said, 'A man may hoard up his money; he may bury his talents in a napkin; but there is one thing he cannot hoard up, and that is love.' You cannot bury it. It must flow out. It cannot feed upon itself; it must have an object."[4]

5. But Jesus waited two more days! This demonstrates that God's plans are often bigger than our plans, and that there is a right timing for God's maximum glory. Jesus understood the power of the resurrection and the appointed timing of Lazarus' and His own death.

E. **John 11:7–10**

1. Jesus' disciples did not initially understand God's plan. So they strongly advised Jesus not to go back to Bethany, which was in Judea where the Jews had tried to stone Him (**verse 8**).

2. In **verses 9–10** Jesus was speaking metaphorically. Daylight represents the knowledge of God's will; whereas, night represents the absence of the knowledge of God's will. When we move in darkness, that is, not knowing God's plan, we are likely to stumble.

   Night or darkness can also be a symbol of life without Christ. Light can be a symbol for life with Jesus, the Light of the World (**verse 9**).

3. Have you noticed Christians whose insufficient knowledge of God's will creates darkness in their lives? Judas was a prime example. After receiving a morsel of bread from Jesus, Judas left to betray Him. **John 13:30** says, **"He went out. And it was night."**

F. **John 11:11–13**

   1. In **verse 11** Jesus said, **"Our friend Lazarus has fallen asleep; but I am going there to wake him up."**

      a. The term **"our friend"** shows the covenant relationship between Christ and each believer. In **John 15:15** Jesus said that He would no longer call His disciples servants, but rather friends.

      b. Death itself does not break this bond of friendship between Christ and a believer. **Romans 8:35, 38–39** establishes this truth. **"Who shall separate us from the love of Christ?...For I am convinced that neither death nor life,...nor anything else in all** creation, will be able to separate us from the love of God that is in Christ Jesus our Lord."

2. It is clear in **verse 12** that the disciples wrongly assumed that Lazarus was physically sleeping and on his way to recovery. Many times Jesus spoke about something and His disciples initially misunderstood His meaning.

3. Following Jesus' ministry on earth, the death of a believer was often referred to as **"sleep"** due to its temporary nature. However, at this point the disciples did not yet understand.

G. **John 11:14–16**

1. **"So then he told them plainly, 'Lazarus is dead…'" John 11:14**. Jesus knew this by revelation from the Holy Spirit—probably the day the messenger came to Him. He told the disciples that for their sake Lazarus' death was a good thing because it would produce an event that would establish their faith even more firmly.

2. What a shocking statement in **verse 15**! Lazarus died so that the disciples might believe! What was it they needed to believe in? Lazarus died so that Jesus' power over death could be shown to His disciples and others.

3. This event was very important because it showed Jesus' power over death. It prepared the disciples for Jesus' death and resurrection. They had seen Jesus raise two other people from the dead—a young girl (**Matthew 9:18–26**) and a widow's

son (**Luke 7:11–18**). Both had been dead for only a short while. Now they would see someone resurrected who had been dead for more than three days.

///

Lazarus' resurrection shows how life in Christ brings victory over the devil's work—sin and death. It is as if Jesus is calling us to come out from sin's enslavement. How do we respond?

///

4. DISCUSS THE ARTICLE **"MANIPULATION, CONTROL AND FEAR OF MAN."** FACILITATE A BRIEF DISCUSSION, ASKING QUESTIONS TO DRAW OUT COMMENTS ABOUT THIS ARTICLE.

H. John 11:17

1. When Jesus arrived at Bethany, Lazarus had been dead in his tomb four days. According to Jewish belief, a dead person's spirit wandered about the sepulcher for three days, seeking an opportunity to return to the body. When decomposition set in on the fourth day, the spirit left because the face of the body was so decayed that it could no longer be recognized.[5]

2. With this viewpoint, resurrection after three days would seem even more impossible. Lazarus' case was unique. Jesus waited until there would be no possibility of explaining away the miracle!

I. John 11:18–24

Lesson 2 — Being Loosed!

1. Martha came out to meet Jesus. She honestly believed that Jesus would have healed her brother if He had been there earlier (**verse 21**).

2. Martha knew of the countless miracles Jesus had done in the past. She had some faith that even now Jesus could do something. She said, **"But I know that even now God will give you whatever you ask"** verse 22.

3. Martha was sure that her brother would be resurrected at the last day with the other dead. She wasn't prepared to fully believe that Jesus would raise Lazarus from the dead now (**verse 24**).

   Do we think, "Someday I will be totally free"? Or can we expect freedom from a besetting sin *today?*

J. John 11:25–27

1. In **John 11:25–26** Jesus made a profound statement! In *The Message* it says, **"You don't have to wait for the End. I am, right now, Resurrection and Life. The one who believes in me, even though he or she dies, will live. And everyone who lives believing in me does not ultimately die at all. Do you believe this?"**

2. These verses make some seemingly paradoxical statements: the believer's death ushers in new life, and the believer has eternal life and will never die spiritually.

3. Then Martha confirmed her belief that Jesus was the Messiah and the Son of God. She is to be commended for her faith. Still, her faith may not

have prepared her for the coming miracle.

K. John 11:28–32

1. Jesus waited to talk to Mary outside of Bethany before going to Lazarus' tomb. (Gravesites were located outside of towns.)

2. Mary found Jesus and fell at His feet. It is interesting that on a previous occasion Mary sat at Jesus' feet (**Luke 10:39**). Later, she washed His feet with ointment (**John 12:3**). Now, totally humbled by a great need, Mary returned to Jesus' feet.

3. Mary's greeting was the same as Martha's. She felt that this tragedy could have been averted if Jesus had been present sooner. Her faith was sincere but limited.

L. John 11:33–34

In *The King James Version*, **verse 33** says that Jesus **"groaned in the spirit, and was troubled."**

1. The word *groaned* is translated from a Greek word that means "to snort with anger, to have indignation."[6]

Why was Jesus angry? Perhaps He was angered at the works of Satan, who had brought sorrow and death to humankind.

Today Jesus is still angered by the works of the enemy in the lives of individuals. Jesus gets just as upset now when He sees the enemy holding His people in bondage.

2. The word *troubled* is translated from a Greek word that means to stir or agitate (like the pool of Bethesda).[7] Jesus' agitation was caused by His hatred of sin, death and Satan.

M. John 11:35–37

1. Jesus then wept. His weeping was different from that of the mourners. His quiet shedding of tears contrasted with their loud wailing. The crowd interpreted His tears as an expression of love, sorrow or perhaps frustration at not being there to heal His dear friend. However, He could have been weeping over the tragic consequences of sin, and how it caused His friends to suffer. He empathized with their suffering.

2. A reflection on Jesus' tears in this passage follows: "The tears of this text are as a spring, a well belonging to one household. The tears over Jerusalem are as a river, belonging to a whole country. The tears upon the cross are as the sea, belonging to the whole world."[8]

N. John 11:38–40

1. Again it says that Jesus was **"deeply moved"** or **"groaned in the spirit (KJV)."** Jesus went to the tomb and commanded that the stone door be removed.

   a. According to Jewish law, anyone touching the tomb's stone door would be defiled. Yet obedience was necessary if Jesus' purposes were to be realized.

> If God's purposes are to be achieved, obedience is required of us as well. This obedience may be difficult or challenging.

      b. The scene was dramatic. The crowd watched and listened. Mary probably wept. Martha protested because ordinarily corpses emit a terrible odor.

      Yet, what "odor" does God endure from us as a result of our sin?

2. The following is an illustration entitled "The Fragrance of His Presence":

Dr. Charles Weigle composed the favorite "No One Ever Cared For Me Like Jesus." One day he visited Pasadena, California. Early that morning he had an opportunity to walk through some of the famous rose gardens when the full fragrance of the flowers filled the air.

Later in the day he arrived at the hotel where a Bible conference was being held. As he took his seat, a man turned to him and said, "Dr. Weigle, I know where you've been. You toured one of our lovely gardens, for I can smell the pleasing aroma on your clothing."

[Dr. Weigle replied,] "My prayer is that I may walk so closely with the Lord that the fragrance of His grace will pervade my being. I want them to know by my words, actions, and songs that I have been with Jesus."[9]

3. Jesus reminded Martha of His earlier promise. If she trusted Jesus and believed His word—that He is the resurrection and the life—God would be glorified (**verse 40**).

O. John 11:41–42

1. Picture the scene as the stone was being rolled away. Imagine the tension. What would Jesus do? This scene was unlike anything that had previously happened in His ministry.

2. Jesus simply thanked His Father for granting His request. He knew He was doing the Father's will in manifesting His love and power.

   a. Jesus' prayer was public—not for the purpose of being known as the Miracle Worker, but so He would be seen as the Father's obedient Son.

   b. The Father's granting of this request would provide clear evidence that Jesus had been sent by Him. This would cause the people to believe in Jesus.

P. John 11:43–44

1. In **John 5:28–29** Jesus said that one day dead men would hear His voice and come out of their graves. And in **John 10:27** Jesus said His sheep hear His voice. Now, following a brief prayer, Jesus called out loudly, **"Lazarus, come out!"** Jesus called Lazarus by name and immediately the dead man came out wrapped in strips of linen cloth! Jesus then directed people to remove the grave clothes so that Lazarus could move on his own, without restriction.

2. Listen to the following illustration:

   As a young man, D.L. Moody was called upon suddenly to preach a funeral sermon. He hunted all through the four Gospels trying to find one of Christ's funeral sermons, but searched in vain. He found that Christ broke up every funeral service He ever attended. Death could not be everywhere He was. When the dead heard His voice, they sprang to life. Jesus said, "I am the resurrection and the life."[10]

3. It is interesting that Jesus involved people in rolling the stone away and unwrapping Lazarus. These actions involved no miracle—just obedient people. Jesus could have miraculously caused the stone to move from its place in front of the tomb. He could have caused the resurrected man to come forth without his grave clothes. Yet Jesus used people to help bring about this spectacular miracle.

   Today, the Holy Spirit is the Miracle Worker, in Jesus' name. We must simply be obedient as He guides us.

4. Lazarus had life, but he needed liberty from his grave clothes. So Jesus called upon those present to free him.

Jesus may call upon us to liberate those who are bound by stinking grave clothes. At times, God may ask us to help set others free from their bondage to sin, enabling them to live in His freedom.

Lesson 2 — Being Loosed!

5. This event is a marvelous picture of Jesus bringing life to people. He not only provides resurrection; He is the Resurrection. He not only gives life; He is the Life.

Q. John 11:45–48

1. Whenever Jesus reveals His identity, it usually produces a discernible response. In this case, we see two different responses. For many Jews, this was clear proof of Jesus' claims and their response was to believe and trust in Him. For others, confusion set in, their hard hearts got harder, and they responded by going to Jesus' enemies to report what had happened.

2. This was such a significant miracle that it caused the Pharisees and Sadducees to call an emergency collaborative meeting. They might have suspected that Jesus was a magician who was trying to deceive the people. They certainly feared a change in the status quo. This miracle made them even more determined to bring about Jesus' death.

3. In **verse 48** it is evident that the chief priests and the Pharisees were walking in the fear of man. They were more worried about what the Jewish people and the Roman authorities thought than about what God thought.

R. John 11:49–53

1. Caiaphas, the high priest that year, was a Sadducee who had been in office for 18 years. As a typical Sadducee, Caiaphas did not believe anyone could be resurrected.

2. READ **JOHN 11:49-53** IN *THE MESSAGE:*

   > Then one of them—it was Caiaphas, the designated Chief Priest that year—spoke up, "Don't you know anything? Can't you see that it's to our advantage that one man dies for the people rather than the whole nation be destroyed?" He didn't say this of his own accord, but as Chief Priest that year he unwittingly prophesied that Jesus was about to die sacrificially for the nation, and not only for the nation but so that all God's exile-scattered children might be gathered together into one people.

3. Inspired by the Holy Spirit, John, the gospel writer, recognized the deep irony in Caiaphas' words. The Chief Priest unwittingly pointed to the sacrificial Lamb of God in a prophecy that he did not even know he was making. Caiaphas meant Jesus had to be killed to maintain the status quo, but God intended to use Jesus' death to save all nations and make them His people (**Ephesians 2:14–18; 3:6**).

S. Conclusion

1. We can learn a lesson from this miraculous event. Our precious Jesus is the One who raises the dead—those who are dead spiritually, as well as those who are dead physically. As He brought the body of Lazarus back from corruption, so He is able and willing to deliver us from our enslaving sins.

2. His life-giving miracle of grace is as truly remarkable as His powerful miracles of

resurrection. What a wonderful King we serve! How fervently Jesus desires us to be totally set free for His glory!

IV. Next Week's Assignment

A. REVIEW NEXT WEEK'S ASSIGNMENT ON THE COURSE OUTLINE.

B. REVIEW THE MAIN PRINCIPLE FOR NEXT WEEK'S LESSON.

C. TELL THE CLASS THAT *ALL* SHOULD PREPARE TO LEAD THE BOOK AND ARTICLE DISCUSSIONS EACH WEEK BEGINNING IN LESSON 4 AND THAT YOU WILL ASK ONE OF THEM TO LEAD THE DISCUSSIONS ONCE YOU ARE TOGETHER IN CLASS.

V. Closing Prayer

END THE LESSON BY PRAYING A CLOSING PRAYER, UNLESS THE LORD INDICATES THAT SOMEONE SHOULD RECEIVE MINISTRY. BE SENSITIVE TO THE HOLY SPIRIT'S GUIDANCE REGARDING HOW TO PRAY. YOU MIGHT WANT TO PRAY WITH THE MAIN PRINCIPLE IN MIND. A SAMPLE PRAYER FOLLOWS:

Dear Lord, thank You for Jesus' sacrifice so that we could be set free from sin. Please reveal to us if we are in bondage to anything. Give us the desire to be free of all enslavement to sin. Help us to be obedient so that we can see Your purposes achieved in our lives. Let our new freedom bring greater honor to You. We pray in Jesus' precious name, Amen.

IN HIS PRESENCE

LESSON 3

UNTIE THE COLT—THE LORD HAS NEED OF IT!

MAIN PRINCIPLE

God has chosen to use people to fulfill His plans and purposes on earth. The Lord wants us loosed from anything holding us in bondage so that we can be free to do what He needs us to do.

WWW.ZOEMINISTRIES.ORG

LESSON 3

Untie the Colt—The Lord Has Need of it!

I. Let's Get Started!

    A. WELCOME THE CLASS AND ENCOURAGE PARTICIPANTS TO BRIEFLY SHARE WHAT GOD HAS DONE IN THEIR LIVES DURING THE PAST WEEK.

    B. OPEN WITH PRAYER.

    C. WORSHIP THE LORD.

    D. HAVE SOMEONE READ THE MAIN PRINCIPLE FOR THIS LESSON.

II. Review

Lessons 1, 2 and 3 are preparation as we enter the last week of Jesus' life. We have seen that the Father desires to have relationship with His children and how that fellowship with God was ruined by the sin of mankind. It is sin that separates us from God. We looked at the story of Lazarus, and how Jesus told the people there to unbind Lazarus from his grave clothes. We were encouraged to examine our hearts, to see what may be binding us and disrupting our relationship with God. In this lesson, we see that the Lord wants us unbound, or loosed, because He has need of us!

Lesson 3 — Untie The Colt—The Lord has Need of It!

III. Supporting Principles From the Book

TIME PERMITTING, ASK ONE PARTICIPANT TO FACILITATE A BRIEF DISCUSSION, ASKING QUESTIONS TO DRAW OUT COMMENTS ABOUT THE ASSIGNED READING. ENCOURAGE THE DISCUSSION LEADER AND PARTICIPANTS TO FOCUS ON PORTIONS OF THE BOOK THAT ARE RELATED TO THE MAIN PRINCIPLE.

IV. Supporting Principles From Scripture—
Luke 19:28–40
Matthew 21:1–11
Mark 11:1–11
John 12:9–19

A. Introduction

1. Most of this discussion will be centered on **Luke 19:28–40**. Portions of the other assigned verses, which are parallel passages to this section of **Luke**, will add to the discussion.

2. Up to this time, Jesus had not sought to be openly called the Messiah. However, now He allowed it and even encouraged it. Everything He did over the course of these next days was designed to call attention to the fact that He is the Messiah!

B. Luke 19:28–29

1. Unlike earthly kings, walking was Jesus' normal mode of transportation. When Jesus and His disciples reached the Mount of Olives, Jesus gave

instructions to two of His disciples. He knew exactly what needed to be done.

2. At this point, Jesus stopped until preparations were made. What timing Jesus had! He fully understood the Father's purposes for Him. Up to this point, Jesus had not tried to make Himself highly visible; on the contrary, He often tried to elude the crowds. It would have been natural to safely slip into Jerusalem unseen and be hidden away in some secret location.

3. When He entered the city in such a publicly obvious way, it was as if He was focusing a spotlight on Himself. He wanted people to know that He was presenting Himself as the Messiah. Jesus' entry into Jerusalem was an act of glorious defiance and courage, because by now the religious leaders were plotting to arrest him (**John 11:57**).

4. It is astonishing that Jesus, knowing that people were seeking to kill Him, still deliberately chose to ride into a city in such a way that every eye was focused on Him. He showed such bravery, or better yet, such confidence in knowing what His Father had called Him to do! One can only believe that this event was carefully planned; this was not just happenstance.

C. Luke 19:30–31

1. In **verse 30** it says, **"You will find a colt tied there, which no one has ever ridden."**

    a. A footnote from *The NIV Study Bible* states:

Luke uses a Greek word that the Septuagint frequently employed to translate the Hebrew word for "donkey." Jesus chooses to enter Jerusalem this time mounted on a donkey to claim publicly that he was the chosen Son of David to sit on David's throne (**1 Ki 1:33,44**), the one of whom the prophets had spoken (**Zec 9:9**).[1]

  b. The two disciples were sent to bring a colt that was probably untamed, since no one had ever ridden on it. It is interesting that an untamed donkey submitted to the Lord more than His own people.

2. It is also interesting that Jesus would send two of His disciples to go into the city to untie that colt. There is a similarity between this account and the account of Lazarus' resurrection. There, Jesus asked "them" to **"take off the grave clothes and let him go" (John 11:44)**. In both cases Jesus used people in very significant events.

3. The words *untie* in **Luke 19:31** and *take off* in **John 11:44** are translated from the same Greek word. To *untie* something is "to loose any person or thing tied or fastened; to release from bonds."[2] To untie can mean to set at liberty.[3]

4. In **Luke 19:31** Jesus said, **"If anyone asks you, 'Why are you untying it?' tell him, 'The Lord needs it.'"** Is something holding us back? Do we need to be set free?

///

We need to be loosed for the benefit of the kingdom of God. As we become more available to the Lord, He will have more freedom to use us to help accomplish His good purposes. Isn't it wonderful to know that the Lord loves and needs us?

///

5. The following scriptural examples of *being loosed* can add to our understanding:

   a. **"And straightway his ears were opened, and the string of his tongue was loosed, and he spake plain" Mark 7:35 (KJV).** *Dake's Annotated Reference Bible* has a footnote that reads, "The string of the tongue was supernaturally cut and also the demon that bound the tongue was cast out. The person was perfectly healed and could now speak plainly and hear clearly in a moment of time."[4]

   b. **"Then should not this woman, a daughter of Abraham, whom Satan has kept bound for eighteen long years, be set free on the Sabbath day from what bound her?" Luke 13:15–16.**

6. In last week's lesson about Lazarus' resurrection, we saw how Jesus was angry at Satan's influence in the world and the effects of sin on the lives of people He loved.

///

It is Jesus' desire that we be freed from all of the enemy's influences, such as the sins of pride or fear of man, which bring death and hinder the work of the Holy Spirit.

///

Lesson 3 — Untie The Colt—The Lord has Need of It

D. Luke 19:32–34

1. The disciples did as the Lord instructed them, and the outcome was just as the Lord had told them to expect. Isn't this always the case? What God says, He does. **Isaiah 55:11** says, **"So is my word that goes out from my mouth: It will not return to me empty, but will accomplish what I desire and achieve the purpose for which I sent it."**

2. In **Mark 11:5–6**, the response of the people standing there was interesting. As the Messiah, He had the right to request whatever He needed. Perhaps Jesus had contacted the owner before this event.

3. The use of a colt or young donkey was highlighted in these verses.

   a. This signaled the fulfillment of a messianic prophecy found in **Zechariah 9:9**. In **Matthew 21:4–5** this prophecy is cited: **"Say to the daughter of Zion, 'See, your king comes to you, gentle and riding on a donkey, on a colt, the foal of a donkey.'"**

   b. The donkey was "symbolic of humility, peace and Davidic royalty."[5] This was not the normal manner in which kings arrived—they usually came as conquerors riding on horses. Yet a donkey, a symbol of peace, accurately represented Jesus, the Prince of Peace.

   c. "By entering into the holy city in this way, Jesus fulfilled prophecy and showed himself to be the true Messiah and Savior, ready to go to the cross and give his life for our sins."[6]

E. Luke 19:35–40

As we read these verses about Jesus entering Jerusalem, our hearts should be preparing for the drama of the final week of Jesus' life.

1. The disciples who procured the donkey threw their garments on it to provide a makeshift saddle (**verse 35**). Many people entered into the excitement of the moment and spontaneously paid tribute to Jesus by spreading out their cloaks on the dusty road before Him. This act of spreading cloaks on the road was a sign of great respect (**verse 36**).

2. The books of **Mark** and **Matthew** state that some people cut leafy branches from nearby trees and fields and spread them on the road. In **John 12:13** palm branches are mentioned.

3. As Jesus headed down the Mount of Olives toward the city, the crowd praised God (**verse 37**). It was the mighty miracles performed by Jesus—the evidences of God's love and spiritual power—that caused the crowd to give God this praise.

4. Here in **Luke 19:37** the people are described as **"the whole crowd of disciples."** In **John 12:12** it says, **"the great crowd that had come for the Feast."** So this was a mixture of Jesus' followers and part of the huge throng that came to Jerusalem for the Passover feast.

Lesson 3 — Untie The Colt—The Lord has Need of It

5. It was customary at the annual Passover festival to chant the six ascent psalms, **Psalms 113–118.** Through these psalms, people expressed thanksgiving, praise and petition to God as they walked up to the temple. (We will discuss the Passover feast next week.)

6. The praises of the crowd came from **Psalm 118:25–26**, one of the ascent psalms. **"O Lord save us; O Lord, grant us success. Blessed is he who comes in the name of the Lord. From the house of the Lord we bless you."**

    a. In **Matthew, Mark** and **John** the crowd is quoted as saying, **"Hosanna!"** and **"Hosanna in the highest!"** *Hosanna* is a Greek word that literally translated means, "Save now!" The early Christian Church later adopted this word into its worship.[7]

    b. In **Matthew, Mark** and **John** they cried out, **"Blessed is he who comes in the name of the Lord!"** In John they also said, **"Blessed is the King of Israel!"** Blessed can mean **"may be blessed."** *The Amplified Bible* also translates *blessed* as **"celebrated with praise."**

    c. The word *Lord* in **"Blessed is he who comes in the name of the Lord!"** is a name that was used for God the Father.[8] So, they were directly associating Jesus with Jehovah, God the Father.

7. One commentary stated, "While the crowd did not fully understand the significance of this event, they seemed to be acknowledging that this One is the promised seed of David who had come to

grant them salvation."⁹ Both the actions and words of the crowd bestowed honor on Jesus, who was presenting Himself as their king at last.

8. The crowd that so exuberantly welcomed their Messiah this day would soon be singing a different tune. They proclaimed His mighty works and powers one moment, and the next considered Him a criminal (**Luke 23:18–23**).

   If we examine our hearts, we see that we can be just as fickle. Without a true heart change, we can be easily caught up in the emotion of the moment. We, too, can be easily ruled by the influence of corrupt leaders.

9. In **Luke 19:39** when the Pharisees said, **"Teacher, rebuke your disciples!"** they understood the significance of what was transpiring. They wanted Jesus to tell His followers to stop calling Him the Messiah and King. Jesus responded that there had to be some proclamation that He was the Messiah. If there wasn't, even inanimate objects like stones would be enabled to testify for Him (**verse 40**).

10. All Jewish history pointed toward this single, spectacular event when the Messiah would publicly present Himself to the Hebrew nation. God wanted this event to be loudly acknowledged!

F. As we begin this journey with Christ, let us open our hearts to a greater revelation of what our Messiah has done for us.

   Here is a fitting story from the *Encyclopedia of 7,700 Illustrations*:

A father had told his son he would send him to sleep in the attic, with only bread and water for his supper, if he broke the laws of the home once more. The child disobeyed again and was sent to the attic. The father could not eat. He had the boy on his mind and his heart. His wife said: "I know what you are thinking. But you must not bring the boy from the attic. It would cause him to disobey again. He would have no respect for your word. You must not cheapen your relation as his father by failing to keep your promise."

To which her husband replied: "You are right. I will not break my word. To do so would cause my son to lose his respect for my word. But he is so lonely up there." He kissed his wife good night, entered the attic, ate bread and water with the boy, and when the child went to sleep on the hard boards, his father's arm was his pillow.

He who knew no sin suffered for the sinner.[10]

V. Discussion of the Assigned Article

TIME PERMITTING, FACILITATE A BRIEF DISCUSSION, ASKING QUESTIONS TO DRAW OUT COMMENTS ABOUT THE ARTICLE.

VI. Next Week's Assignment

A. REVIEW NEXT WEEK'S ASSIGNMENT ON THE COURSE OUTLINE.

B. REVIEW THE MAIN PRINCIPLE FOR NEXT WEEK'S LESSON.

C. THE FACILITATOR WILL FACILITATE THE SCRIPTURE DISCUSSION. REMIND THE CLASS THAT NEXT WEEK YOU WILL ASK SOMEONE TO LEAD THE BOOK OR ARTICLE ASSIGNMENT. SO, ALL SHOULD BE READY TO LEAD THESE DISCUSSIONS.

VII. Closing Prayer

END THE LESSON BY PRAYING A CLOSING PRAYER, UNLESS THE LORD INDICATES THAT SOMEONE SHOULD RECEIVE MINISTRY. BE SENSITIVE TO THE HOLY SPIRIT'S GUIDANCE REGARDING HOW TO PRAY. YOU MIGHT WANT TO PRAY WITH THE MAIN PRINCIPLE IN MIND. A SAMPLE PRAYER FOLLOWS:

Lord Jesus, we praise You for being our Messiah and King! Thank You for desiring to have us participate in Your exciting work on earth. Reveal to us anything that keeps us bound in sin. Free us so that we may be available for Your service. In Your name we pray, Amen.

IN HIS PRESENCE

LESSON 4

JESUS, OUR PASSOVER LAMB

MAIN PRINCIPLE

We can come to God only because of the atoning work of Christ, our Passover Lamb. As His blood covers us by faith, we can abide in God's glory.

LESSON 4

Jesus, Our Passover Lamb

I. Let's Get Started!

A. WELCOME THE CLASS AND ENCOURAGE PARTICIPANTS TO SHARE WHAT GOD HAS DONE IN THEIR LIVES THIS PAST WEEK.

B. OPEN WITH PRAYER.

C. WORSHIP THE LORD.

D. HAVE SOMEONE READ THE MAIN PRINCIPLE FOR THIS LESSON.

II. Supporting Principles From the Book

TIME PERMITTING, ASK ONE PARTICIPANT TO FACILITATE A BRIEF DISCUSSION, ASKING QUESTIONS TO DRAW OUT COMMENTS ABOUT THE ASSIGNED READING. ENCOURAGE THE DISCUSSION LEADER AND PARTICIPANTS TO FOCUS ON PORTIONS OF THE BOOK THAT ARE RELATED TO THE MAIN PRINCIPLE.

III. Discussion of the Assigned Article "God So Loved the World"

REQUEST ONE PARTICIPANT TO FACILITATE A BRIEF DISCUSSION, ASKING QUESTIONS TO DRAW OUT COMMENTS ABOUT THIS ARTICLE.

Lesson 4 — Jesus, Our Passover Lamb

ENCOURAGE THE DISCUSSION LEADER AND PARTICIPANTS TO FOCUS ON PORTIONS OF THE ARTICLE THAT ARE RELATED TO THE MAIN PRINCIPLE.

IV. Supporting Principles From Scripture—Matthew 26:1–5 Exodus 12:1–28

A. Matthew 26:1–5

1. At the time of this passage, Jesus had been warning His disciples for the last six months about His impending death. In this passage He indicated when and how He would be killed—during the celebration of the Passover feast by crucifixion (**verse 2**).

2. Passover was a spring festival that coincided with the barley harvest in March and April. In the later years of Jesus' life, He regularly went to Jerusalem for the Passover (**John 2:13**). This feast was associated with the historical event of Israel's departure from Egypt.

3. Israel's exodus from Egypt is viewed as the greatest redemptive event under the old covenant found in the Old Testament. The exodus foreshadowed Jesus Christ and the redemption He brings under the new covenant.

4. In **verses 3–5** we see the treachery and guilt of the Jewish religious leaders. These are the priests who regularly offered to God the blood of lambs in atonement for the sins of the people. Now they

were preparing to sacrifice Jesus, not understanding the full impact of their plan.

5. They didn't dare arrest and kill Jesus during Passover, which preceded the weeklong feast of Unleavened Bread (**Exodus 12:6, 18**). During this feast, the population of Jerusalem increased from 50,000 to several hundred thousand people.[1] Such crowds were easily excitable and many people deeply admired Jesus. The Jewish religious leaders planned to kill Jesus before the feast of Unleavened Bread. According to Jewish customs, each day began at sundown. The feast of Passover began on the evening of the 14th day of the month of Nisan (ni´-san), also called Abib (aw-beeb´).

6. Because Jesus accurately predicted the day He would be killed, we are assured that God was in complete control of the upcoming events.

7. Jesus would, of His own free will, be killed as the sacrificial Passover Lamb on the 14th day of the month of Nisan and, thereby, fulfill all the Old Testament prophecies and foreshadowing.

B. Exodus 12:1–28

1. **Background**

   At this point in time, the Jews had been in bondage to the Egyptians for 400 years. However, God was determined to honor His covenant and deliver the descendants of Abraham, Isaac and Jacob. God raised up Moses to deliver the Israelites from the slavery of Pharaoh. Under the direction and leading of God, Moses confronted Pharaoh and conveyed

Lesson 4 — Jesus, Our Passover Lamb

God's message: **"Let my people go, so that they may worship me" Exodus 8:20.** Through Moses, God manifested His great power, giving Pharaoh many chances to relent. Then God told Moses that He would send a final plague—one that would kill the firstborn of every family in Egypt (**Exodus 11:4–7**).

2. In **verse 2** the Lord said, **"This month is to be for you the first month, the first month of your year."**

The *NIV Study Bible* comments, "This was the inauguration of the religious calendar in Israel. In the ancient Near East, new year festivals normally coincided with the new season of life in nature. The designation of this month as Israel's religious New Year reminded Israel that her [new] life as the people of God was grounded in God's redemptive act in the exodus."[2]

The Passover when Jesus died was the beginning of our current calendar as well, with Jesus' crucifixion marking the years to come as A.D. (anno Domini), the year of our Lord.

3. **Verses 3–5**

   a. In **verse 3** the Lord instructed them to **"take a lamb."** Each person had to eat a portion of the lamb (**verse 4**), just as each person today must personally receive Jesus, the Lamb, in order to receive salvation.

   b. The head of each family was to sacrifice a lamb (**verses 3–4**). Think of the projected outcome of this command for the entire nation of Israel.

> According to Josephus (Wars VI. 9, 3) ten persons was the least number, and twenty the greatest permissible number of persons who could partake of a single Passover lamb. If one lamb was slain for fifteen persons on an average throughout the nation, then for two and one half million people at the time of the Exodus, over 160,000 lambs were slain on the historic night when the bonds of Egypt gave way before the blood.[3]

c. The animal must be a year old male lamb or kid without defect (**verse 5**). The words *without defect* come from the Hebrew word *tamiym* (tah-meem´), which means without blemish, complete, full, perfect, sound, without spot, undefiled, upright, whole.[4]

d. This lamb without defect is a type and shadow of Jesus Christ, the perfect Son of God. The following scriptures underline this fact:

Hebrews 9:14 says, **"Christ, who through the eternal Spirit offered himself unblemished to God...."**

1 Peter 1:19 says, **"but with the precious blood of Christ, a lamb without blemish or defect."**

2 Corinthians 5:21 says, **"God made him who knew no sin to be sin for us, so that in him we might become the righteousness of God."

4. **Verses 6–7, 13, 27—The significance of the blood**

   a. The purpose of the blood applied on the Jewish homes' doorframes was to save each family's firstborn son from death. The angel of death was not allowed to enter the homes that had the blood painted on the doorposts.

   b. God has *always* required blood to be shed in atonement for sin. **Hebrews 9:22b** says, **"Without the shedding of blood there is no forgiveness."**

      - "At the beginning of creation, God commanded that living creatures, greatly beloved of Adam, must be slaughtered by him and their blood must be shed to supply a covering for Adam and Eve's obvious nakedness. Fig leaves were insufficient. So animals were slaughtered and after the blood was shed, Adam and Eve were covered with the skins. The principle of a life for a life runs throughout the Bible. No other garments would sufficiently cover Adam and Eve except those which involved the shedding of blood."[5]

      - The Lord had Noah take more than one pair of every clean animal on the ark. These animals were to be used for making offerings to God (**Genesis 8:20**).

- God had promised Abraham that from his seed would come a nation. Yet he was asked by God to offer Isaac, his only son, on the altar. Abraham willingly obeyed, knowing from his relationship with Jehovah, that God would supply a substitute offering or resurrect Isaac (**Genesis 22:8**).

- God spoke to Moses in **Leviticus 17:11, "For the life of a creature is in the blood, and I have given it to you to make atonement for yourselves on the altar; it is the blood that makes atonement for one's life."**

The significance of Jesus' blood is that through it alone we are eternally saved from death and God's wrath against sin.

5. **Verses 8–10**

    a. "Jews were to roast the lamb and not eat any of it raw, as Egyptians who ate raw flesh in honor of Osiris…Thus God was seeking in every conceivable way to make Israel free from all idolatrous practices and honor to any false god."[6]

    b. The bitter herbs would bring to mind for the Israelites the bitter time of slavery in Egypt, since endive, chicory and other bitter-tasting plants naturally grew there.[7]

    c. The Israelites were to eat bread made without yeast—unleavened bread—commemorating the rushed evacuation of Egypt, which left no time for unbaked bread to rise.

Lesson 4 — Jesus, Our Passover Lamb

6. **Verse 11** describes how the Israelites were instructed to eat this meal: **"…with your cloak tucked into your belt, your sandals on your feet and your staff in your hand. Eat it in haste; it is the Lord's Passover."**

   a. Eating the Passover feast while wearing traveling clothes was a sign of the Hebrews' faith. Though they were not yet free, they were preparing themselves for travel. Because God had promised He would lead them out of Egypt, their preparation was an act of faith.

   Preparing ourselves for the fulfillment of God's scriptural promises, however unlikely they may seem, demonstrates our faith.

   b. Compare these items of clothing and tools with some of the clothing and tools recommended for Christians in **Ephesians 6:14–17.**

   "Your cloak tucked into your belt" can be equated with the belt of truth. "Your sandals on your feet" is similar to feet shod with the preparation of the gospel of peace **(KJV)**. "Your staff in your hand" is like the sword of the Spirit, which is the word of God.

   We need to have this attitude of obedience and faith, enabling us to move quickly at God's request.

7. **Verses 12–13 "I will bring judgment on all the gods of Egypt. I am the Lord. The blood will be a sign for you on your houses where you are; and when I see the blood, I will pass over you.**

No destructive plague will touch you when I strike Egypt."

Egypt is a symbol for evil and sin. God was making clear His sovereignty over all evil (**verse 12**).

Because of our relationship to Jesus and the protection provided by His blood, we should not fear opening our hearts to God, allowing death to come to those things that don't belong in our hearts.

---

8. **Verses 14–28**

    a. In **verses 14, 17** and **24** God commanded His people to commemorate this day as a lasting ordinance. The Israelites celebrated the Passover as a remembrance of their deliverance from bondage and death in Egypt.

    The act of eating the lamb caused the Israelites to associate the lamb's death with the great compassion of the Lord, who spared them from physical death.

    b. According to **Hebrews 10:1**, this feast was a **"shadow of the things that were to come."** The Passover served to foreshadow Jesus shedding His blood and delivering us from bondage, death and sin! Now we observe the Lord's supper in remembrance of Jesus' death, recalling how His sacrifice spared us from condemnation and spiritual death.

    In **1 Corinthians 11:23b–25** Jesus commands us to **"Do this in remembrance of me."**

In **1 Corinthians 10:16–17** Paul asked, **"Is not the cup of thanksgiving for which we give thanks a participation in the blood of Christ? And is not the bread that we break a participation in the body of Christ?"**

c. In **verses 14–20** God commanded the Israelites to remove all yeast from their houses. In Scripture, yeast often represents sin and corruption (**1 Corinthians 5:6–8**). The unleavened bread would remind the Israelites that God had brought them out of slavery because they were His chosen people, intentionally separated from the world and from sin.

d. **Verses 22–23** describe what they were to do with the blood of the lamb. The presence of that blood would protect the Israelites. **Verse 23b says, "He will not permit the destroyer to enter your houses and strike you down."**

We Christians may also protect our households from the enemy through applying the blood of Jesus by faith. We can pray, "In Jesus' name I place the blood of Jesus over my home and family."

e. In **verse 27** the Israelites responded to God's deliverance by worshiping the Lord for His saving grace. God brought the Israelites out of Egypt, not because they were exceptionally worthy, but because He loved them and He was faithful to the covenant He had made with Abraham (**Deuteronomy 7:7–10**).

We worship the Lord, knowing that the salvation we enjoy through Jesus is not based on our worthiness. It is because of God's faithfulness, love and amazing grace.

V. The Exodus and Jesus' Fulfillment of the Requirements of the Feast of Passover

A. SHARE THE FOLLOWING SUMMARY WITH THE CLASS. REFER THEM TO THE STUDY HELP **"THE LAMB OF GOD"** IN THE STUDY GUIDE.

The following summary is derived from Richard Booker's *Jesus in the Feasts of Israel*, pp. 18–28.[8]

In **Isaiah 53** the prophet predicted that a human "lamb" would give his life in order to deal with the problem of sin and death, once and for all. In fulfillment of the feast of Passover and Isaiah's prophecy in **Isaiah 53:7**, Jesus **"was oppressed and afflicted, yet He did not open His mouth; he was led like a lamb to the slaughter" verse 7.** The prophet John the Baptist said of Jesus, **"Look, the lamb of God, who takes away the sin of the world!" John 1:29.**

In **Exodus 12:43–48** God continued to give His people instructions on how to be saved from the final plague He was sending on Egypt. Let's examine God's instructions along with the requirements that Jesus fulfilled when He represented the Passover Lamb.

Lesson 4 — Jesus, Our Passover Lamb

Jesus was set aside to be sacrificed, examined and crucified on the exact month, days and hours that the Jews were preparing and sacrificing their Passover lambs.

1. During the exodus on the tenth day of the month of Nisan, every man was supposed to select a male lamb without spot or blemish.

   Jesus entered Jerusalem on the tenth day of the month of Nisan, to be set aside as the human "lamb" **(John 12:1,12–13)**.

2. During the exodus, each man was to observe this lamb for five days, to be certain there was nothing wrong with it.

   Jesus was observed and tested by the religious leaders for five days. They questioned His authority and asked Him trick questions, hoping He would give a wrong answer with which they could accuse Him. They could not find anything wrong with Him **(Matthew 21:23–27; Matthew 22:15–46)**. Even Pilate, after interrogating Jesus, said in **John 19:4, "I find no fault in him" (NKJ)**.

3. During the exodus on the fourteenth day of Nisan at twilight, each man was to bring the lamb to his doorstep and kill it, catching some of its blood in a basin.

   In Jesus' day, people brought their lambs to Jerusalem or they purchased Temple lambs for sacrifice. Because there were many thousands of lambs, it was necessary for the Jews to prepare them for sacrifice at nine a.m. on the fourteenth. They then killed them at three p.m. so the Passover meal could begin by six p.m., which they considered the beginning of the next day.

Jesus was crucified on the fourteenth day of the month of Nisan. He was nailed to a cross at nine a.m. (the third hour by Jewish time) (**Mark 15:25**). At three p.m. (the ninth hour), Jesus died (**Mark 15:33–37**).

4. Each man was to sprinkle the lamb's blood on both sides of the doorpost and above the doorpost. His family was to enter their house through the bloodstained door and remain there. If the entrance of a house was covered by blood, the angel of death could not enter, but had to *pass over* that house.

Jesus shed His blood so that we would be spared the penalty for our sins.

5. The Israelites in Egypt were to roast the lamb on a spit shaped like a crossbar, being careful not to break any of its bones.

Jesus' bones were not broken. When the soldiers came to break His legs to hasten His death, they found that He had already died (**John 19:31–33**).

6. The Israelites were to eat the whole lamb, not leaving any of it until the next day.

The Jews hurriedly took Jesus' body down before the Sabbath began at twilight, so He was not left on the cross until the next day. Jesus gave His all as the final Passover sacrifice on the fourteenth of Nisan (**John 19:31**).

7. No uncircumcised man could eat the Passover meal. The only people who could celebrate this feast were those who accepted, and were in covenant with, the Hebrew God as the one true God.

We are reconciled to God when we acknowledge Jesus as our substitute sacrifice (**Ephesians 2:13**). This is the first step in knowing God and walking with Him. When we accept Jesus as our personal Lord and Savior, we come into covenant with God and can enjoy the blessings that come with knowing Him. We can come into God's presence only by being covered by Jesus' blood.

B. Personal Application

1. Today the feast of the Passover reminds us of how God has delivered each of us from the bondage of sin and death.

2. Even though we deserve death as the penalty for our sin (**Romans 3:23; Romans 6:23**), God made a way for us to be saved. Jesus' blood cleanses us from all sin (**1 John 1:7**).

3. When we apply Jesus' blood to the doorposts of our hearts, death cannot hold us. We no longer need to fear death, because the resurrection of Jesus and our coming resurrection have taken away death's sting (**1 Corinthians 15:51–57**).

AS CLASS MEMBERS READ FURTHER IN **MATTHEW 26**, SOMEONE MAY QUESTION THE VALIDITY OF THE TIMING CITED IN COMPARING THE PASSOVER PREPARATIONS WITH JESUS' CRUCIFIXION.

THERE IS SOME CONTROVERSY AMONG SCHOLARS REGARDING WHETHER THE LAST SUPPER WAS A PASSOVER MEAL AND WHETHER IT WAS EATEN BEFORE THE REGULARLY SCHEDULED PASSOVER MEAL. EITHER WAY, IT IS WIDELY ACCEPTED THAT JESUS DID FULFILL ALL THE REQUIREMENTS OF A PASSOVER LAMB. DISCUSSION OF THIS CONTROVERSY WOULD BE GETTING OFF TRACK AND SHOULD BE AVOIDED.

VI. Discussion of the Assigned Article

TIME PERMITTING, REQUEST ONE PARTICIPANT TO FACILITATE A BRIEF DISCUSSION, ASKING QUESTIONS TO DRAW OUT COMMENTS ABOUT THE ARTICLE.

VII. Next Week's Assignment

A. REVIEW NEXT WEEK'S ASSIGNMENT ON THE COURSE OUTLINE.

B. REVIEW THE MAIN PRINCIPLE FOR NEXT WEEK'S LESSON.

C. THE FACILITATOR WILL FACILITATE THE SCRIPTURE DISCUSSION. REMIND THE CLASS THAT NEXT WEEK YOU WILL ASK SOMEONE TO LEAD THE BOOK OR ARTICLE ASSIGNMENT. SO, ALL SHOULD BE READY TO LEAD THESE DISCUSSIONS.

VIII. Closing Prayer

END THE LESSON BY PRAYING A CLOSING PRAYER, UNLESS THE LORD INDICATES THAT SOMEONE SHOULD RECEIVE MINISTRY. BE SENSITIVE TO THE HOLY SPIRIT'S GUIDANCE REGARDING HOW TO PRAY. YOU MIGHT WANT TO PRAY WITH THE MAIN PRINCIPLE IN MIND. A SAMPLE PRAYER FOLLOWS:

Thank You, Lord, for being our Passover Lamb and delivering each of us from the bondage of sin and death. Open our eyes and hearts to see afresh what You did for us at Calvary. Deepen our understanding of our personal need for grace. Thank You that our salvation is based on Your faithfulness, love and amazing grace, and not on our worthiness. Forgive us for trying to come to You through our own self-righteousness.

Please forgive us for letting sin and worldly ways cause our first love for You to grow cold. Rekindle our first love for You, Lord. Work in our hearts so we acknowledge You alone as our source of security. Help us to obey You and ignore distracting voices. Create in us a burning desire to set aside time every day in which to seek You, Lord. We pray in Jesus' precious name, Amen.

IN HIS PRESENCE

LESSON 5

BETRAYAL VERSUS LOVE

MAIN PRINCIPLE

God wants us to extend extravagant love toward Jesus. Are we willing to give to Jesus anything He asks us of us because He laid down His life for us? Are we willing to lay down our own plans and ambitions for Him? Are we willing to show our love for Jesus despite what people will think?

LESSON 5

Betrayal Versus Love

I. **Let's Get Started!**

    A. WELCOME THE CLASS AND ENCOURAGE PARTICIPANTS TO SHARE WHAT GOD HAS DONE IN THEIR LIVES THIS PAST WEEK.

    B. OPEN WITH PRAYER.

    C. WORSHIP THE LORD.

    D. HAVE SOMEONE READ THE MAIN PRINCIPLE FOR THIS LESSON.

II. **Supporting Principles From the Book**

    ASK ONE PARTICIPANT TO FACILITATE A BRIEF DISCUSSION, ASKING QUESTIONS TO DRAW OUT COMMENTS ABOUT THE ASSIGNED READING. ENCOURAGE THE DISCUSSION LEADER AND PARTICIPANTS TO FOCUS ON PORTIONS OF THE BOOK THAT ARE RELATED TO THE MAIN PRINCIPLE.

III. **Supporting Principles From Scripture—**
    Matthew 26:6–35
    Mark 14:3–26

    A. Matthew 26:6–13 (Mark 14:3–9)

Lesson 5 — Betrayal Versus Love

1. The location of this incident was Bethany, in the home of Simon the Leper. At one time Simon had been a leper and was evidently healed by Jesus.

2. Bethany was the home of Jesus' close friends—Mary, Martha and Lazarus. In this gospel, the woman in **verse 7** is unidentified, but in **John 12:1–11** it mentions Lazarus' sister, Mary, by name.

3. In **Matthew 26:7** Mary approached Jesus as He was reclining at the table. "In Palestine people did not sit to eat, they reclined on low couches. They lay on the couch resting on the left elbow and using the right hand to take their food. So then anyone coming up to someone lying like this would stand well above them."[1]

4. It was also customary for the men to eat separately from the women, who were often in the kitchen cooking. Having a woman present during this meal was definitely improper and probably quite shocking for those in attendance.

5. Bible commentator William Barclay describes Mary's actions in the following way:

   > To Jesus there came a woman with an alabaster phial of ointment. It was the custom to pour a few drops of perfume on a guest when he arrived at a house or when he sat down to a meal. This phial held nard, which was a very precious ointment made from a rare plant that came from far-off India. But it was not a few drops that this woman poured on the head of Jesus. She broke the flask and anointed him with the whole contents.[2]

6. This woman loved Jesus for what He had done for her personally. She loved Him for what He had done for her brother. She loved Him for who He was—joyful, tender, sensitive to the needs of others, morally strong, full of authority, and self-controlled when provoked by evil men. She was willing to use all her costly perfume in order to express her love and respect for Jesus.

///

Because of how Jesus rescued us from our former lives, what He has done for our families and who He is, we also need to put our love for Jesus *into action*.

///

7. As God gives us deeper intimacy with Jesus, we need to respond by giving Him more of ourselves—the sin in our lives for His cleansing, our time with Him in worship and prayer, our talents for His use. Jesus poured out His life for us. Shall we think anything too precious to pour out upon Him?

8. Mary anointed Jesus' head. She was willing to risk embarrassment to anoint Jesus in that way. Would we be willing to act in such an "inappropriate" way if it would honor Jesus?

9. If you want to rattle "religious" people, do something out of the ordinary for Jesus, and you will see their true heart attitudes surface.

We see this with the disciples, especially Judas. They all said, **"Why this waste?... This perfume could have been sold at a high price and the money given to the poor" Matthew 26:8–9**. In **John 12:6** we see that Judas was the most upset. **"He** [Judas]

Lesson 5 — Betrayal Versus Love

did not say this because he cared about the poor but because he was a thief; as keeper of the money bag, he used to help himself to what was put into it."

10. Jesus defended Mary in **Matthew 26:10: "Why are you bothering this woman? She has done a beautiful thing to me."** Jesus answered them by quoting from **Deuteronomy 15:11a—"There will always be poor people in the land."** This was not a justification for ignoring the needs of the poor; rather Jesus said this to highlight the special sacrifice Mary made for Him.

11. Christ recognized Mary's act to be one of great faith as well as great love. Jesus said, **"She did it to prepare me for burial" Matthew 26:12.** Though the disciples ignored Christ's many predictions of His approaching death (**Matthew 16:21; 17:22; 20:18**), apparently this woman believed Jesus.

12. **Matthew 26:13** shows that Jesus knew His death would not stop the spread of the good news of reconciliation with God the Father. "The cross loomed close ahead now, but He never believed that the Cross would be the end. He knew that the good news would go all round the world. And with the good news there went the story of this lovely thing, done with love's reckless extravagance, done on the impulse of the moment, done out of a heart of love."[3]

Mary exemplified a selfless love for Jesus. We need to love Jesus in that way—where our fear of others' disapproval does not prevent us from openly, whole-heartedly loving Him.

13. What kind of love do we extend toward Jesus? Is our love for Jesus extravagant? Are we willing to lay down everything for Jesus just as He laid down His life for us? Are we willing to give up our careers, our finances, our own agendas for our children if He asks that of us?

B. Matthew 26:14–16

Here extravagant love is contrasted with extreme selfishness. It is interesting that these two incidents are situated together, showing us the vivid contrast of different relationships with Jesus!

1. We know from **verse 14** that Judas went to the chief priests, not vice versa. His betrayal of Jesus was premeditated.

2. **Luke 22:1–6** says that Satan entered Judas before he went to the chief priests and officers and discussed with them how he might betray Jesus. Just as God looks for men and women to be His vessels, so does Satan. We can be instruments for good or evil.

3. **"...I have set before you life and death, blessings and curses. Now choose life, so that you and your children may live and that you may love the Lord your God, listen to his voice, and hold fast to him. For the Lord is your life..." Deuteronomy 30:19–20.** Satan could not enter Judas unless he gave Satan access. It is our choice to open our heart to death (Satan) or life (Jesus Christ). Judas chose the former.

4. What were his reasons?

Lesson 5 — Betrayal Versus Love

    a. *Greed and covetousness* were definitely involved. Judas asked what price the authorities were willing to pay. He was the treasurer of the group and used his position to pilfer from the common purse (**John 12:6**).

    b. *Disappointment and bitterness* may have played a part. Jesus did not do what Judas wanted Him to do. Judas wanted Jesus, as Messiah, to overthrow the Romans, who occupied Israel by force. He wanted Jesus to use His power to establish a just Jewish government, of which Judas would have an important part.

    c. *Ambition and jealousy* were also probable cause. "In reality Judas attached himself to Jesus, not so much to become a follower of Jesus, as to use Jesus to work out the plans and desires and schemes of his own ambitious heart."[4]

    In **Luke 22:24** the account of the Last Supper included an argument among the disciples as to who was the greatest of them. If the other disciples were caught up in such an argument, surely Judas would have joined in.

5. Do we ever fall prey to these temptations? Do we love money and our possessions more than God? Do we allow ourselves to get disillusioned and bitter when God doesn't do what we thought He should do? Do we have grandiose plans in which we are lifted up and admired?

We need to see past our perceived needs and plans and recognize that God's ways are not our ways

(**Isaiah 55:8**). His plan will be much better than any plan we could devise (**Ephesians 3:20**).

///

We need to set aside our pride and ambition, walk in humility and seek to cooperate with God's plans. Then God will lift us up in due time (**Luke 14:11**).

///

C. Matthew 26:17–25; Mark 14:12–21

ENCOURAGE PARTICIPANTS TO KEEP A FINGER IN BOTH PASSAGES.

1. Mark 14:12–16

   a. Jesus' disciples (**Luke 22:8** specifies Peter and John) asked where they were to make preparations for the Passover. Jesus told them to go into the city and find a man carrying a jar of water. This man would have looked conspicuous in the crowds since carrying water was ordinarily a woman's job. They were to follow him and tell the owner of the house, **"The Teacher asks: Where is my guest room, where I may eat the Passover with my disciples?" Mark 14:14.** We see here that Jesus was an organizer and planner. It appears He made arrangements with the man beforehand.

   b. The disciples obeyed Jesus and found things just as He had described to them. They prepared the Passover meal—unleavened bread, wine, bitter herbs, sauce and the lamb (**Mark 14:16**).

   c. THERE IS SOME CONTROVERSY AMONG THEOLOGIANS ABOUT

Lesson 5 — Betrayal Versus Love

WHETHER JESUS ACTUALLY ATE A PASSOVER MEAL. HOWEVER, DISCUSSING ALL THIS WOULD NOT BE KEEPING TO THE MAIN PRINCIPLE OF THIS LESSON, WHICH ENCOURAGES US TO EXAMINE WHAT KIND OF LOVE WE SHOW TOWARD JESUS, AND WHETHER WE LET THE FEAR OF MAN OR SELFISH AMBITIONS SQUELCH OUR LOVE FOR HIM. IF YOU NEED TO OFFER SOME EXPLANATION TO YOUR CLASS, FOLLOWING FIND A BRIEF EXPLANATION OF DIFFERING VIEWS.

- Some say that the Last Supper was not a Passover meal because Jesus was killed as our Passover Lamb at the same time the priests were sacrificing the Passover lambs. They say that the disciples had prepared a Passover meal to be enjoyed later.

- Others believe that the disciples prepared the Passover meal a day early so that Jesus could enjoy the Passover meal with them.[5]

- Some maintain there was a disagreement that year between the Pharisees and Sadducees about when the new moon was seen, which indicated the first day of the month of Nisan. Jesus could have eaten the Passover meal a day early on what the Pharisees claimed was the right day.[6]

- Others claim that the Last Supper was a regular Passover meal, not taking into account that Jesus died at 3 p.m. on the 14th of

Nisan, the same time that the lambs were sacrificed.[7]

AVOID UNNECESSARILY WASTING CLASS TIME ON THESE THEORIES. THE ENDNOTES INCLUDE SOME SUGGESTED REFERENCES THAT YOU COULD SHARE WITH ANYONE INTERESTED IN FURTHER STUDY.

2. **Mark 14:17–21**

   a. The new Jewish day began at 6 p.m. That evening Jesus dined with His disciples, reclining at the table (**Mark 14:18**). This is unlike the Passover meal in Egypt, where the Israelites ate their meal standing up, ready for a quick departure. Here we see a more relaxed atmosphere.

   With preparations being made for the Passover, the disciples probably had a renewed awareness of God's desire to save His people. They were probably warmed by thoughts of being part of a special community, not only God's chosen people, Israel, but also Jesus' chosen disciples.

   b. What a shock it must have been to hear Jesus say, **"I tell you the truth, one of you will betray me—one who is eating with me" verse 18.** We can't help but realize that Jesus knew exactly what was ahead of Him.

   c. In **verse 19** the disciples began questioning Jesus, **"Surely not I?"** In **John 13:24–25** Peter told John to ask Jesus to identify the betrayer.

d. Jesus responded, **"It is one of the Twelve,... one who dips bread into the bowl with me"** verse 20.

- "It was the custom—still practiced by some in the Middle East—to take a piece of bread, or a piece of meat wrapped in bread, and dip it into a bowl of sauce (made of stewed fruit) on the table...In that culture, as among Arabs today, to eat with a person was tantamount to saying, 'I am your friend and will not hurt you.' This fact made Judas's deed all the more despicable."[8]

- At this point Jesus may have recalled **Psalm 41:9** and may have related closely with David, the psalm writer, who wrote, **"Even my close friend, whom I trusted, he who shared my bread, has lifted up his heel against me."**

e. **"But woe to that man who betrays the Son of Man! It would be better for him if he had not been born" verse 21.** There would be catastrophic consequences for Judas' betrayal of Jesus.

There are consequences for us when we betray Jesus. *How could we betray Jesus?*

- The Holy Spirit asks you to tell an unbeliever what Jesus means to you, but you remain silent.

- You hold a grudge against a fellow Christian, criticize him in conversation with another and refuse to see Christ in him.

- Someone in authority ridicules Christianity and the Holy Spirit tells you to stand up and be counted as a Christian, but you keep your beliefs private.

- You let your own ambitions and desire for approval override your relationship with Jesus.

f. Now we'll switch to Matthew's account. In **Matthew 26:25** Jesus said, **"But woe to that man who betrays the Son of Man."** Judas specifically asked Jesus, **"Surely not I, Rabbi?" Then Jesus answered him, "Yes, it is you."** Jesus tried to save Judas from carrying out his plan!

g. Even though Jesus knew what lay ahead of him, He offered Judas the opportunity to receive His love again. Jesus had done this time and again. Jesus' character matched His Father's—slow to anger, compassionate, desirous that none should perish (**Numbers 14:18; 2 Peter 3:9**).

h. But Jesus' love could not reach Judas' heart. Judas remained unmoved, even after Jesus gave him the opportunity to correct his attitude and change his plan.

i. This truly depicts what happens to a person who has hardened his heart to the things of God; the outcome will always be death. William Barclay explains it this way:

> Without a doubt Jesus could forcibly have stopped Judas. All He had to do was tell the other eleven what Judas was meditating and

planning, and Judas would never have left that room alive that night, for the others would have murdered him rather than let him go. Here is the whole human situation. God has given us wills that are free. His love appeals to us. His truth warns us. But there is no compulsion. It is the awful responsibility of man that he can spurn the appeal of God's love, and disregard the warning of God's voice. In the end there is no one but ourselves responsible for our sins.[9]

Judas chose to proceed with his plan. He left the light, life and love of the presence of Jesus and went out into the night, according to **John 13:30**. It is always dark when someone turns his back on God.

3. **Matthew 26:26–30**

Jesus knew that the time of His death was near (**John 13:1**) and He took every opportunity to prepare His disciples for His death and what it would mean.

a. **"...Jesus took bread, gave thanks and broke it, and gave it to his disciples, saying, 'Take and eat; this is my body'" Matthew 26:26.**

The bread represented Jesus' body, which would be broken for us.

b. **"Then he took the cup, gave thanks and offered it to them, saying, 'Drink from it, all of you. This is my blood of the covenant,** which is poured out for many for the forgiveness of sins'" Matthew 26:27–28.

- The wine in the cup represents Jesus' blood, His "poured-out life."[10] Jesus wanted His disciples to know that the shedding of His blood would establish a new blood covenant between God and man. Anyone who accepted Jesus' substitutionary death for their sins would receive forgiveness of sins—past, present and future.

- We can benefit from this blood covenant now when we recognize its eternal effectiveness. We can claim all the benefits of that covenant now as we bring that covenant back to mind. For example, we can claim God's protection of us through Jesus' shed blood and Satan has to retreat and honor that blood as our covering.

- "The new covenant was a relationship between man and God which was not dependent on law but on love. In other words Jesus says, 'I am doing what I am doing to show you how much God loves you.' Men were no longer simply under the law of God. Because of what Jesus did and came to tell, they were forever with the love of God. That is the very essence of what the sacrament says to us."[11]

- The Greek word for *give thanks* here is *eucharistia* (yoo-khar-is-tee´-ah), which means giving thanks to God as an act of worship.[12] The term eucharist is derived from this word.

Lesson 5 — Betrayal Versus Love

The meaning of eucharist expresses the correct response to Jesus' gift of His body and blood—thanksgiving and worship of God.

c. **Verse 30** says that they sang a hymn and then went to the Mount of Olives. This worship of God the Father may have helped Jesus put His human emotions into submission to God's will.

4. **Matthew 26:31–35**

   In this passage Peter's denial of Jesus is predicted. Peter, in his zealousness, was determined to stand by Jesus.

   a. In **Luke 22:31–32** Jesus said, **"Simon, Simon, Satan has asked to sift you as wheat. But I have prayed for you, Simon, that your faith may not fail. And when you have turned back, strengthen your brothers."**

   b. Both Peter and Judas betrayed Jesus. However, we see quite a contrast in the heart attitudes of Peter and Judas. Though Peter denied Jesus, he was passionately devoted to Him.

   c. Peter betrayed Jesus because he was too afraid of what people would say or do if they knew He was Jesus' disciple. His sin was that he walked in the fear of man instead of in the fear of the Lord. However, unlike Judas, Peter's love for Jesus caused him to repent. And once he repented, he strengthened the other disciples.

   d. According to **Romans 8:1**, there is no condemnation in Christ Jesus. When we fail—

which will happen—we can repent and again be used by God to help others. It is said, "It is better to follow and fail than fail to follow."

IV. Discussion of the Assigned Article

TIME PERMITTING, ASK ONE PARTICIPANT TO FACILITATE A BRIEF DISCUSSION, POSING QUESTIONS TO DRAW OUT COMMENTS ABOUT THIS ARTICLE. ENCOURAGE THE DISCUSSION LEADER AND PARTICIPANTS TO FOCUS ON PORTIONS OF THE ARTICLE THAT ARE RELATED TO THE MAIN PRINCIPLE.

V. "Open Arms"

READ ALOUD TO THE CLASS MAX LUCADO'S "OPEN ARMS" OF *NO WONDER THEY CALL HIM THE SAVIOR.*

VI. Next Week's Assignment

A. REVIEW NEXT WEEK'S ASSIGNMENT ON THE CLASS OUTLINE.

B. REVIEW THE MAIN PRINCIPLE FOR NEXT WEEK'S LESSON.

C. THE FACILITATOR WILL LEAD THE SCRIPTURE DISCUSSION. REMIND THE CLASS THAT NEXT WEEK YOU WILL ASK SOMEONE TO LEAD THE BOOK OR ARTICLE ASSIGNMENT. SO, *ALL* SHOULD BE READY TO LEAD THESE DISCUSSIONS.

VII. Closing Prayer

END THE LESSON BY PRAYING A CLOSING PRAYER, UNLESS THE LORD INDICATES THAT SOMEONE SHOULD RECEIVE MINISTRY. BE SENSITIVE TO THE HOLY SPIRIT'S GUIDANCE REGARDING HOW TO PRAY. YOU MIGHT WANT TO PRAY WITH THE MAIN PRINCIPLE IN MIND. A SAMPLE PRAYER FOLLOWS:

Thank You, Father, for Your willingness to send Your Son so that we could have a love relationship with You. Thank You, Jesus, for Your willingness to lay down Your life for us. Work in our hearts so that our love for You will be rekindled. Make us willing to put aside anything that impedes our receiving Your love. Give us extravagant love for You. Make us willing to give You anything in our life that You ask of us. Show us if there is anything in our life that is keeping us from loving You fully—fear of disapproval from others, lack of trust in You or other specific sins. In Jesus' precious name, Amen.

IN HIS PRESENCE

LESSON 6

DECISIONS—STAGE ONE

MAIN PRINCIPLE

As we see Jesus pray in anguish in the Garden of Gethsemane and allow Himself to be arrested, we need to decide if we are willing to follow in Jesus' footsteps. Are we willing to follow Jesus and put our relationship with the Father first in our lives, even if it means going toward the cross and laying down everything for our Lord?

LESSON 6

Decisions—Stage One

I. Let's Get Started!

    A. WELCOME THE CLASS AND ENCOURAGE PARTICIPANTS TO BRIEFLY SHARE WHAT GOD HAS DONE IN THEIR LIVES DURING THIS PAST WEEK.

    B. OPEN WITH PRAYER.

    C. WORSHIP THE LORD.

    D. HAVE SOMEONE READ THE MAIN PRINCIPLE FOR THIS LESSON.

II. "The Part That Matters"

READ ALOUD TO THE CLASS THIS CHAPTER FROM MAX LUCADO'S BOOK *NO WONDER THEY CALL HIM THE SAVIOR*. THIS IS OPTIONAL, IF TIME PERMITS.

III. Supporting Principles From the Book

ASK ONE PARTICIPANT TO FACILITATE A BRIEF DISCUSSION, ASKING QUESTIONS TO DRAW OUT COMMENTS ABOUT THE ASSIGNED READING. ENCOURAGE THE DISCUSSION LEADER AND PARTICIPANTS TO FOCUS ON PORTIONS OF THE BOOK THAT ARE RELATED TO THE MAIN PRINCIPLE.

IV. Supporting Principles From Scripture— Matthew 26:36–56 Mark 14:32–50 Luke 22:39–53

A. Review

The following Scripture study serves as a review of Lessons 1–5 and as an introduction to Lessons 6–12.

HAVE THE CLASS TURN TO **HEBREWS 12:1–4**, AND TEACH THE FOLLOWING:

1. **"...Let us throw off everything that hinders and the sin that so easily entangles..." Hebrews 12:1.**

    a. In previous lessons we have looked at how God created us for relationship with Him, but that Adam and Eve's original sin separated us from God's presence.

    b. We looked at the distractions and sins in our lives that *hinder* and *entangle* us and too often keep us from entering into His presence.

Lazarus was raised from the dead, but he still had on grave clothes that needed to be removed. In another account, the disciples were told to untie a donkey because "the Lord has need of it."

///

Christ wants us loosed, untied, disentangled and unhindered because He has need of *us!*

///

2. **"Let us fix our eyes on Jesus..." verse 2.**

   a. Now, and in following lessons, we will focus on Jesus by examining the final week of His life. We will study, sometimes in explicit detail, the surrender, suffering, endurance, humiliation and death of Jesus.

   b. **Verse 2** also says, **"who for the joy set before him endured the cross."** It makes us wonder. What was the joy that was set before Jesus—a joy so compelling that it inspired Him to endure the cross?

   We suggest a possible answer to this question. Perhaps God set before Jesus His pure, spotless Bride—the Church—as the "reward" for His sacrifice.

   This concept is a prelude to another ZOE course—*How to Know God's Voice—In the Coming of the Lord*.

3. **"Consider him who endured such opposition... resisted to the point of shedding...blood..." verses 3–4.**

   In the coming lessons we will examine the 10 stages of Christ's shedding of blood. We will go from the Garden of Gethsemane, where He sweated great drops of blood, to the beating, humiliation, scourging, crowning with thorns, crucifixion, and, finally, the spear piercing His side.

4. Conclusion

We will see the veil, symbolizing our former separation from God, being torn in two. We will see a way opened for us to enter into *God's very presence* by the blood of the Lamb!

B. The Beginning of Christ's Suffering in the Garden of Gethsemane—Matthew 26:36–37

1. In **verse 36** we see Jesus and His disciples heading toward the Garden of Gethsemane after they had eaten the Last Supper together.

2. As Jesus walked with His disciples to Gethsemane, a deep sadness was probably already developing in Jesus' heart. The reality of His approaching death undoubtedly bore down upon Him. Jesus' prophecy about the disciples betraying Him still hung heavy in the air.

3. In **Luke 22:39** it says, **"Jesus went out as usual to the Mount of Olives, and his disciples followed him."** This is where Gethsemane was located. Prior to this, Jesus must have spent considerable time praying here. This is how Judas knew where to take the Roman soldiers.

4. Jesus was heading into a time of prayer in a place with a significant name. The name Gethsemane means "oil press, a place for squeezing the oil from olives."[1] Jesus went there to press into God in prayer, which He did until drops of sweat and blood pressed out of Him.

5. Jesus said to His disciples, **"Sit here while I go over there and pray."** It is interesting that Jesus left eight of the disciples, giving no other

instructions but to sit while He prayed (**verse 36**). Jesus took James, John and Peter along with Him as He prayed and gave them special instructions (**verse 37**).

///
As we become closer and more intimate with Jesus, more is required of us!
///

6. As Jesus took these three with Him and prayed, He began to feel overwhelmingly sorrowful and troubled. Jesus wanted His closest friends to be near Him at this difficult time. Jesus was foreseeing the separation from His Father that He would endure as He took on the sin of the world. The separation from His Father was too much to bear alone; Jesus wanted to be with those who loved Him.

7. **"The Fog of the Broken Heart"**
   READ ALOUD TO THE CLASS THIS CHAPTER FROM MAX LUCADO'S *NO WONDER THEY CALL HIM THE SAVIOR.*

SHARE WITH THE CLASS THE SECTION BELOW ABOUT THE STAGES

INTRODUCTION TO THE STAGES

WE HAVE JUST COMPLETED FIVE WEEKS OF INTRODUCTION TO THE LAST WEEK OF JESUS' LIFE. THE CURTAIN HAS OPENED FOR THE FINAL ACT, SCENE ONE, OR AS WE CALL IT, STAGE ONE.

AS WE ADVANCE TOWARD THE VICTORIOUS DAY OF THE CROSS, AND PONDER EACH

STAGE, LET US NEVER TAKE OUR EYES OFF THE REASON JESUS CAME TO THIS EARTH. LET US CLOSELY EXAMINE OUR HEARTS WITH EACH STAGE AND ASK OURSELVES, "DO I REALLY UNDERSTAND AND BELIEVE IN THE MIRACLE OF JESUS' CONCLUDING DAYS ON EARTH?" LET'S ACKNOWLEDGE IN OUR HEARTS THE IMPORTANCE OF EACH STEP JESUS TOOK TOWARDS THE CROSS. PLEASE DON'T ALLOW THIS TO BE ONLY A MENTAL ASSIGNMENT, BUT WELCOME THE WORK OF THE HOLY SPIRIT TO MAKE THIS A *LIFE-CHANGING ASSIGNMENT FROM HEAVEN*. LET US ONCE AGAIN RETURN TO OUR FIRST LOVE (**REVELATION 2:4**)!

WE ARE NOW IN STAGE ONE—IN ANGUISH JESUS CHOSE TO OBEY THE FATHER.

WE NEED TO DECIDE. ARE WE WILLING TO FOLLOW IN JESUS' FOOTSTEPS? ARE WE WILLING TO FOLLOW JESUS EVEN IF IT MEANS GOING TOWARD THE CROSS AND LAYING DOWN EVERYTHING FOR GOD?

C. MATTHEW 26:38–39

1. In **verse 38a** Jesus expressed the pain and turmoil that He was feeling: **"My soul is overwhelmed with sorrow to the point of death."**

    a. It was Jesus' soul, or *psuche* (psoo-khay´) in Greek, that was in distress. His mind, will and emotions were overwhelmed.

    b. In *The Amplified Bible* Jesus said, **"My soul is very sad and deeply grieved, so that I am almost dying of sorrow. Stay here and keep awake and keep watch with Me."**

    c. The word *sorrow* is translated from the Greek word *lupeo* (loo-peh´-o), which means distress, grief or heaviness.[2]

2. In **verse 38b** Jesus said, **"Stay here and keep watch with me."**

    a. *Keep watch* in **verse 38** means to refrain from sleep; to give strict attention to, to be cautious, to take heed lest through remissness some calamity suddenly overtake one.[3]

    Jesus said *watch* three times in verses **38–41**.

    b. Earlier that day Jesus had said that His disciples would disown Him, and they protested that they would die for Him. Now Jesus asked them to keep watch and stay awake with Him, yet they could not watch with Him one single hour! (**verse 40**).

We need to *keep watch*—to be continually alert, aware, and discerning, remembering to look with our spiritual eyes. Then we will trust, and sometimes understand what God is doing, especially in times of trial.

The Lord is saying to us, "Sit with Me, and watch with Me. Know My ways and what I am doing among you." We need to be alert, aware of the schemes of the enemy, full of faith, and ready to pray and take action.

3. **"Going a little farther, he fell with his face to the ground and prayed, 'My Father, if it is possible, may this cup be taken from me. Yet not as I will, but as you will'" verse 39.**

   a. Jesus' course was set, but being fully human, He struggled. Because of the anguish He faced, Jesus can relate to us when we struggle.

   b. Jesus was in great distress over what lay ahead. In **verse 39**, in the phrase **"may this cup be taken from me,"** what did Jesus mean by the term **"this cup"**?

      - Was He acutely aware of the pain to come—physical, emotional and mental?

      - Was Jesus dreading the thought of being spiritually separated from His Father as He took on the sin of the world?

      - Was Jesus feeling pain for the suffering His disciples would soon experience as they betrayed and abandoned Him and then grieved His absence?

   c. *The Fire Bible* gives one explanation:

      What Christ meant by "this cup" has been the subject of much discussion and debate. (1) It is doubtful that Christ was praying to be saved from physical death because that was the reason he came to earth. He had prepared his entire life to finish that mission and die for the sin of humanity...(2) It is more likely that Jesus was praying to be spared from the agony of separation from God the Father—that separation being the ultimate penalty for sin—which he would have to endure as he literally took the guilt and punishment of all sin upon himself (see 2 Cor. 5:21)... However, Jesus prayed, "nevertheless, not as I will, but as you will." He then committed himself to endure both physical death and spiritual separation from his heavenly Father in order to obtain and guarantee our spiritual salvation...It is apparent that the Father heard his prayer and gave him strength to drink the bitter "cup" he was destined to receive (see Heb. 5:7).[4]

d. In **Mark 14:36**, Jesus began this prayer with, **"Abba, Father."** *Abba*, roughly meaning Daddy, shows the intimacy Jesus had with the Father.

e. Obedience to the Father was supremely important to Jesus! Jesus said, **"But the world must learn that I love the Father and that I do exactly what my Father has commanded me" John 14:31.** His strength to obey came from His relationship with God. The Son's love for the Father enabled Him to say, in effect, "I will do whatever You want. I don't want to be out of Your will."

Like Jesus, we also gain strength from spending time in the presence of the Lord.

D. Discussion of the Assigned Article

ASK ONE PARTICIPANT TO FACILITATE A BRIEF DISCUSSION, POSING QUESTIONS TO DRAW OUT COMMENTS ABOUT THIS ARTICLE. ENCOURAGE THE DISCUSSION LEADER AND PARTICIPANTS TO FOCUS ON PORTIONS OF THE ARTICLE THAT ARE RELATED TO THE MAIN PRINCIPLE.

We need to prioritize spending time with God as our highest responsibility and privilege.

e. Matthew 26:40–42

READ ALOUD **MATTHEW 26:40–42** FROM THE MESSAGE:

"When he came back to his disciples, he found them sound asleep. He said to Peter, 'Can't you stick it out with me a single hour? Stay alert; be in prayer so you don't wander into temptation without even knowing you're in danger. There is a part of you that is eager, ready for anything in God. But there's another part that's as lazy as an old dog sleeping by the fire.'"

1. "Then he returned to his disciples and found them sleeping. 'Could you men not keep watch with me for one hour?' he asked Peter" verse 40.

    a. Jesus must have prayed for a full hour, seeking guidance and strength to accomplish God's purposes!

///

> Do we give God enough time in which to speak to us
> and work in our hearts while we pray?

///

    b. **Verse 40b** in *The King James Version* reads, **"What! Could ye not watch with me one hour?"** *What* in this verse conveys a forcefulness in Jesus' question. It is as if Jesus was exasperated to see them unaware of the importance of their praying.

    c. Jesus was struggling with what lay ahead—the betrayal, arrest, trial, crucifixion and separation from the Father—things to which He had alluded during His earthly ministry. The disciples had seen Mary anoint Jesus for burial. They had heard Him talk of His body and blood during the Last Supper. They had heard Jesus speak of being betrayed by one of them. And now his closest friends (even John) were too sleepy to keep watch in this time of need?

    Yet, are we any different? We, too, are often not vigilant, not responsive to God or those deeply hurting around us.

    d. Jesus specifically addressed Peter here. Jesus knew the temptation Peter would face (to deny knowing Jesus because of his fear of man). Peter especially needed to hear what Jesus said next.

2. **"Watch and pray so that you will not fall into temptation. The spirit is willing, but the body is weak" verse 41.**

a. If he could have stayed awake long enough to pray, prayer would have helped Peter meet that temptation. Prayer would have helped all the disciples avoid giving in to the temptation to flee.

b. In His mercy, Jesus recognizes that our physical bodies and our human wills are weak, making it sometimes difficult to obey God, even when our spirits want to obey Him.

3. **"He went away a second time and prayed, 'My Father, if it is not possible for this cup to be taken away unless I drink it, may your will be done'"** verse 42.

Again Jesus begins His prayer with **"My Father,"** calling on the One He was sure would help Him.

F. MATTHEW 26:43–44

1. **"When he came back, he again found them sleeping, because their eyes were heavy"** verse 43.

    a. Their full stomachs, the wine at dinner and the late hour must have made it difficult for the disciples to stay awake.

    Do we fail to pray as we should for the people God has laid on our hearts? Do we give up praying too soon, either due to fatigue or failure to understand what gets accomplished when we pray? Thankfully, Jesus intercedes for us continually at the right hand of the Father, so that when we fail, He perseveres and triumphs.

b. Perhaps we also deal with a spiritual counterpart to "heavy eyes"—eyes that are not seeing the need to pray, or are not discerning specifically how God wants us to pray.

2. **"So he left them and went away once more and prayed the third time, saying the same thing" verse 44.**

   Jesus was still struggling with His soul, wrestling to obey what the Father was asking. However, Jesus continued turning to the Father in prayer. He kept talking to His Father about it, confessing His reluctance but pledging His obedience.

   We often *avoid* talking with God when we are struggling to obey Him, and our souls are tempted to avoid something difficult.

   ///

   Like Jesus, we need to keep turning to God in prayer when we are having trouble obeying Him. Prayer will help us keep our will in line with God's will.

   ///

3. **Luke 22:43 says, "An angel from heaven appeared to him and strengthened him."**

   a. Jesus asked His loyal disciples to watch with Him during this time of agony. However, the lack of support and ministry from His disciples had to be supplied angelically as He endured this agony.

   b. Once the angel had strengthened Jesus, apparently He was able to pray more earnestly.

Lesson 6 — Decisions—Stage One

We sometimes become so preoccupied and busy that we forget to turn to God and seek His presence. Therefore, we become overwhelmed and succumb to weariness. If only we would take the time to pull into the presence of God, the Holy Spirit would strengthen us.

4. **Luke 22:44** says, **"And being in anguish, he prayed more earnestly, and his sweat was like drops of blood falling to the ground."**

   a. Jesus' struggle in prayer intensified over time. The phrase **"being in anguish"** or **"being in an agony,"** as it is translated in *The King James Version*, is written in Greek in the aorist participle. This suggests a growing intensity in Jesus' struggle.

   b. The struggle for Jesus was so intense that even His sweat had blood in it. *Dake's Annotated Reference Bible* comments: "It is a recognized fact that under extreme mental pressure, the pores may be so dilated that the blood may issue from them; so that there may be bloody sweat. A number of cases are on record of such agony."[5]

   c. Barclay helps us see this agony from God's perspective:

   The Greek word [for agony] is used of someone fighting a battle with sheer fear. There is no scene like this in all history. This was the very hinge and turning point in Jesus' life. He could have turned back even yet. He could have refused the Cross. The salvation of the world hung in the balance as the Son of God literally sweated it out in Gethsemane; and he won.[6]

G. "Then he returned to the disciples and said to them, 'Are you still sleeping and resting? Look, the hour is near, and the Son of Man is betrayed into the hands of sinners. Rise, let us go! Here comes my betrayer!'" Matthew 26:45–46.

   1. "The hour is near" refers to the time of the event for which Christ came into the world—His death—in order to reconcile us back to Abba, Father.

   2. What courage Jesus displayed here! His time spent with the Father gave Him the ability to victoriously obey.

H. Matthew 26:47–49

   1. "Now the betrayer had arranged a signal with them: 'The one I kiss is the man; arrest him.' Going at once to Jesus, Judas said, 'Greetings Rabbi!' and kissed him" verses 48–49.

   The Greek word for *kissed* indicates more than a casual greeting. Judas gave to Jesus the affectionate and fervent greeting of an intimate friend. William Barclay comments: "When a disciple met a beloved Rabbi, he laid his right hand on the Rabbi's left shoulder and his left hand on the right shoulder and kissed him. It was the kiss of a disciple to a beloved master that Judas used as a sign of betrayal."[7]

   2. How could Judas do this?

Judas was deceived into believing that Jesus was going to usher in the kingdom of God through use of God's power. Judas wanted to force Jesus' hand and make it happen immediately. Judas' rebellion left him vulnerable to Satan's deception. Judas had it so fixed in his mind as to how it should happen that he ignored what Jesus had been showing him. Jesus had ridden into Jerusalem on a colt, indicating humility. Jesus had washed the disciples' feet, modeling servanthood.

We can be deceived in the same way; our minds can be so set on things happening a certain way that we fail to discern God's desires and intentions.

I. **Matthew 26:50–56**

1. **"Jesus replied, 'Friend, do what you came for'" verse 50a.** The term *friend* is translated from a Greek word that means companion, comrade or partner.[8] Jesus' love for Judas continued even to the end.

2. READ **JOHN 18:4–11**, WHICH CONTAINS ADDITIONAL INFORMATION.

    a. John 18:4–5a reads, "Jesus, knowing all that was going to happen to him, went out and asked them, 'Who is it you want?' 'Jesus of Nazareth,' they replied. 'I am he,' Jesus said,...When Jesus said, 'I am he,' they drew back and fell to the ground."

    Jesus' words, **"I am he,"** are reminiscent of the name God gave Moses to tell the Israelites—**"I AM WHO I AM"** (Exodus 3:14). This was the name of the God who was going to deliver them. At this point, Jesus was revealing His awesome deity.

Their fall to the ground indicates that Jesus could have used His divine power to prevent His arrest. This was a lesson to the disciples that He could have escaped if it was not His appointed time to return to the Father.[9]

   b. In **John 18:10** we read that Peter took a sword and struck the ear of the high priest's servant. In **Luke 22:51** we read that Jesus healed the ear. Jesus, with a momentarily free hand, touched and healed the cut ear of a man coming to arrest Him. This miracle was performed without any request or exercise of faith from the servant. This shows the kind of love with which Jesus operated. This was Jesus' last miracle before dying on the cross, where He healed the sin-wound of our lost world.

3. TURN BACK TO **MATTHEW 26:50–56**.

In **Matthew 26:53** Jesus said, **"Do you think I cannot call on my Father, and he will at once put at my disposal more than twelve legions of angels? But how then would the Scriptures be fulfilled that say it must happen in this way?"**

   a. *The NIV Study Bible* states that one legion consisted of 6,000 soldiers.[10] So, 12 multiplied by 6,000 would make 72,000 angels that Jesus could muster to His aid at a moment's notice.

   b. The Scripture to which Jesus referred was **Zechariah 13:7**. This verse predicted that all the disciples would flee and desert Him, which they did (**verse 56**).

Even after Jesus declared that He could call upon His Father to send 12 legions of angels, His disciples fled when they perceived that He intended to quietly yield Himself to the soldiers. Their courage and boastful resolutions quickly failed, and Jesus' words were thus fulfilled.

4. **Conclusion**

   Although the disciples' conduct cannot be excused, we can certainly learn from them. Unlike them, we must keep watch, spend time in God's presence, and allow God to prepare our hearts for what is ahead. We need to be ready to risk all to follow Jesus, even if it means going toward the cross and dying to self.

V. Next Week's Assignment

   A. REVIEW NEXT WEEK'S ASSIGNMENT ON THE COURSE OUTLINE.

   B. REVIEW THE MAIN PRINCIPLE FOR NEXT WEEK'S LESSON.

   C. THE FACILITATOR WILL FACILITATE THE SCRIPTURE DISCUSSION. REMIND THE CLASS THAT NEXT WEEK YOU WILL ASK SOMEONE TO LEAD THE BOOK OR ARTICLE ASSIGNMENT. SO, ALL SHOULD BE READY TO LEAD THESE DISCUSSIONS.

VI. CLOSING PRAYER

END THE LESSON BY PRAYING A CLOSING PRAYER, UNLESS THE LORD INDICATES THAT SOMEONE SHOULD RECEIVE MINISTRY. BE SENSITIVE TO THE HOLY SPIRIT'S GUIDANCE REGARDING HOW TO PRAY. YOU MIGHT WANT TO PRAY WITH THE MAIN PRINCIPLE IN MIND. A SAMPLE PRAYER FOLLOWS:

Thank You, Jesus, for what You endured in the Garden of Gethsemane. Thank You for pressing through in prayer and remaining obedient to the Father. Please forgive us for the times that we have deserted or denied You. Help us to remain watchful and responsive to You, whether it is in prayer for others or in communing with You.

Help us make time spent in Your presence our top priority, knowing that it is the only way for You to do the necessary work in our hearts. Please enable us to be willing to lay down everything in order to follow You faithfully. In Your name we pray, Amen.

IN HIS PRESENCE

LESSON 7

HUMILIATION—STAGE TWO

MAIN PRINCIPLE

As we read of Jesus silently enduring being mocked, spat upon and beaten, we realize that He suffered this humiliation for our sake. He did this so that we would be able to come into the fullness of relationship with Him. Are we willing to stand firm in our belief in Jesus, desire only His approval, and endure humiliation for Him?

WWW.ZOEMINISTRIES.ORG

LESSON 7

Humiliation—Stage Two

I. Let's Get Started!

    A. WELCOME THE CLASS AND ENCOURAGE PARTICIPANTS TO BRIEFLY SHARE WHAT GOD HAS DONE IN THEIR LIVES DURING THE PAST WEEK.

    B. OPEN WITH PRAYER.

    C. WORSHIP THE LORD.

    D. HAVE SOMEONE READ THE MAIN PRINCIPLE FOR THIS LESSON.

II. Discussion of Assigned Article "Fill Us With Your Passion, Lord!"

ASK ONE PARTICIPANT TO FACILITATE A BRIEF DISCUSSION, POSING QUESTIONS TO DRAW OUT COMMENTS ABOUT THIS ARTICLE. ENCOURAGE THE DISCUSSION LEADER AND PARTICIPANTS TO FOCUS ON PORTIONS OF THE ARTICLE THAT ARE RELATED TO THE MAIN PRINCIPLE.

III. Supporting Principles From the Book

ASK ONE PARTICIPANT TO FACILITATE A BRIEF DISCUSSION, ASKING QUESTIONS TO DRAW OUT COMMENTS ABOUT THE ASSIGNED READING.

ENCOURAGE THE DISCUSSION LEADER AND PARTICIPANTS TO FOCUS ON PORTIONS OF THE BOOK THAT ARE RELATED TO THE MAIN PRINCIPLE.

IV. Supporting Principles From Scripture—Matthew 26:57–75
Luke 22:54–65
John 18:12–27

A. Review

Today's Scriptures depict the second point where Jesus was afflicted. The first point of Jesus' suffering was when He prayed in the Garden of Gethsemane. There, Jesus was face-down on the ground, sweating bloody sweat. The intensity increased each time He returned to prayer. Finally, Jesus was strengthened and He chose to obediently do what His Father had sent Him to accomplish.

B. Introduction

1. In **John 18:12–14,19–24** we see that Jesus was first brought before Annas, the father-in-law of Caiaphas, the presiding high priest that year. Annas was a notorious character who was full of corruption. Annas and his family had become wealthy by making it difficult for the Jews to offer the unblemished sacrifices they brought from outside the Temple. "Outside the Temple a pair of doves could cost as little as 9d [denarii]; inside it they could cost as much as 15s [shekels]." The sacrifices brought from the outside were always found to be blemished. Therefore, the worshiper

would have to purchase another sacrifice. Annas was behind this extortion![1]

2. William Barclay continues, "Now we can see why Annas arranged that Jesus should be brought first to him. Jesus was the man who had attacked Annas' vested interest; Jesus was the man who had cleared the Temple of the sellers of victims, and who had hit Annas where it hurt—in his pocket and his bank account. Annas wanted to be first to gloat over the capture, the defeat, the discomfiture of this disturbing Galilean."[2]

3. Because Jesus had upset the corrupt status quo of those in power, much of the humiliation they inflicted was motivated by revenge.

C. Matthew 26:57–58

1. Jesus was taken before some of the members of the Sanhedrin (**verse 57**).

   The Sanhedrin was "the high court of the Jews. In NT times it was made up of three kinds of members: chief priests, elders, and teachers of the law. Its total membership numbered 71, including the high priest, who was presiding officer. Under Roman jurisdiction the Sanhedrin was given a great deal of authority, but they could not impose capital punishment.... "[3] The Sanhedrin's responsibility was to prepare a charge, so that a criminal could be tried before the Roman governor. Caiaphas, the high priest, presided over this court.

So, that night Caiaphas and his cohorts tried to prepare a charge against Jesus that would merit the death penalty by the Roman governor.

2. Peter followed Jesus **"at a distance" verse 58**. Because of his fear, Peter was reluctant to be associated with Jesus. An attitude of denial was already forming. Peter was waiting to see the outcome.

3. In **John 18:15–16** we learn that John was known to the high priest. John, the writer of that gospel, was **"the other disciple."** John used his influence to gain Peter's entry into the high priest's courtyard.

D. Matthew 26:59–61

1. Because Jesus was blameless (like a Passover lamb), the chief priests and members of the Sanhedrin were looking for false evidence with which they could justify Jesus' execution (**verse 59**).

   If they could prove that Jesus had taught blasphemy and false doctrine, they would have something legitimate against him.

2. To build a case, they needed the testimony of two or three witnesses, according to Jewish law (**Numbers 35:30; Deuteronomy 17:6; 19:15**). Finally they found two false witnesses, who misquoted what Jesus had said (**John 2:19: "Destroy this temple, and I will raise it again in three days."**). Jesus' words were also misinterpreted, as Jesus had spoken of His body when referring to the temple.

3. Satan, the father of lies, always misuses Scripture. Remember how Satan tempted Jesus in the wilderness and used Scripture in his attempt to interfere with Jesus' mission. But this time, Jesus remained silent.

4. Here the religious leaders were about to destroy Jesus' body, just as He had said, and three days later He would rise from the dead!

E. **Matthew 26:62–64**

1. Jesus held His peace—not as self-condemned or in confusion—so that **Isaiah 53:7** might be fulfilled: **"He was oppressed and afflicted, yet he did not open his mouth; he was led like a lamb to the slaughter, and as a sheep before her shearers is silent, so he did not open his mouth."** Because His final hours were at hand, remaining silent was a wise and obedient response.

   At any time, Christ could have called upon God, and legions of angels would have come to His defense.

2. When Christ was made sin for us, He was silent and left it to His blood to speak the final word (**Hebrews 12:24**).

3. In **verse 63** Caiaphas said to Jesus, **"I charge you under oath by the living God: Tell us if you are the Christ, the Son of God."** According to Jewish law (**Leviticus 5:1**), people were required to testify if they had pertinent knowledge regarding a public legal charge. They had to disclose evidence or be held personally responsible if they withheld

information. Caiaphas' public charge required Jesus to speak the truth, even though it was incriminating.

How ironic that Caiaphas charged Jesus under oath by the **"living God"**! Jesus is the Living God!

4. Imagine the intensity of this scene. The Jewish nation had been waiting hundreds of years for the Messiah's arrival. Now Caiaphas asked openly if Jesus was the Christ (**verse 63**).

5. The high priest was so determined to entrap Jesus and pronounce the penalty of death that he could not recognize the true Messiah. It was as if scales were covering his eyes. Pride, malice and jealousy will blind people and propel them into deeper sin!

6. Jesus had seldom openly confessed His identity as the Messiah, the Son of God. His message and miracles indicated it, but now He professed it publicly (**verse 64**)!

7. Jesus spoke with assurance, courage and determination, for He was confident of the end results: **"Yes, it is as you say…But I say to all of you: In the future you will see the Son of Man sitting at the right hand of the Mighty One and coming on the clouds of heaven"** verse 64.

   a. **"Sitting at the right hand of the Mighty One and coming on the clouds of heaven"** fulfilled messianic prophesies from **Psalm 110:1** and **Daniel 7:13**.

   b. Jesus spoke of His coming in a cloud in power to His disciples for their comfort in **Luke**

21:27–28. Here Jesus spoke of it to His enemies as a warning.

  c. In *The New King James* translation, **verse 64** says that Jesus would be sitting at the right hand of **"the Power."** This word is translated from the Greek word *dunamis* (doo´-nam-is), which means miraculous power, strength, might or great force.[4] It can be used to describe divine power overcoming all resistance.

8. In obedience to the Father, Jesus now refrained from overtly using His power. Jesus knew that by remaining passive then, He would become the perfect sacrifice, through which God's divine power would overcome Satan's resistance to God's will.

F. Matthew 26:65–66

1. In **verse 65** the high priest tore his clothes, according to the Jewish custom when they heard or saw anything said or done that they considered a reproach to God.

2. The elders agreed with Caiaphas, and sentenced Jesus to death. They said, **"He is worthy of death" verse 66**. Jesus was proclaimed "worthy of death" by these priests, just as a Passover lamb was offered up as a worthy sacrifice. Thus our Lord was condemned to die, so that through His sacrifice we might live (**John 10:28**).

3. The religious leaders refused to even consider that Jesus' words might be true. Condemning him to death, they set themselves on the road to death as well.

People are no different now. When they refuse to confess Jesus Christ as the Messiah, the Son of God, they sentence themselves to hell, eternal separation from *Abba*, Father!

WE ARE NOW IN STAGE TWO— JESUS ENDURED HUMILIATION.

Jesus was willing to be spit upon and mocked. He endured humiliation for us.

G. Matthew 26:67–68

1. Those in attendance spit in His face, thereby fulfilling Scripture. **Isaiah 50:6b says, "I did not hide my face from mocking and spitting."**

2. Spitting in the face was considered the most degrading insult one could give (**Numbers 12:14; Deuteronomy 25:9; Job 30:10**). Yet Christ submitted to it on behalf of humankind.

3. They blindfolded Him (**Mark 14:65**) and struck Him with their fists (**Matthew 26:67**). By this, Scripture was again fulfilled (**Isaiah 50:6** and **Lamentations 3:30**).

4. Having first blindfolded Christ, they challenged Him to prophesy who struck Him. This demonstrated the great depravity of human nature. They mocked the Son of God's prophetic office, saying, **"Prophesy to us, Christ. Who hit you?" verse 68**.

H. Matthew 26:69–75

1. In **verse 68** the Sanhedrin mockingly commanded Jesus to prophesy. In **verses 69–75** Jesus' prophecy was fulfilled when Peter denied Him. See also **Luke 22:54–62** and **Mark 14:66–72.**

2. Surrounded by danger, overwhelmed with terror and tempted by Satan, Peter was challenged as a follower of Jesus. If Peter had stayed awake and spent more time in prayer with God, perhaps he would have been better prepared for this challenge.

3. However, now Peter forgot all the promises of Jesus. His denial came in three stages.

    a. **"You also were with Jesus of Galilee" verse 70.** In response to this charge, Peter acted confused, saying, **"I don't know or understand what you're talking about" Mark 14:68.** He walked away in an attempt to remove the focus on himself.

    b. **"This fellow was with Jesus of Nazareth" verse 71.** Peter vehemently denied Jesus, this time with an oath: **"I don't know the man!" verse 72.**

    c. **"Surely you are one of them, for your accent gives you away" verse 73.**

        Verse 74 reads, **"Then he began to call down curses on himself and he swore to them, 'I don't know the man!'"** This was the worst of all. One did this kind of swearing in a court of law. Peter swore that he did not know Jesus and invoked a curse on himself if his words were untrue. In effect, he was saying, **"May God strike me dead if I am lying."**

4. There was a progression to Peter's denial to which we also can be susceptible. First, he allowed fear and unbelief to rise up his heart, and he turned away from Jesus. With each successive confrontation his heart became more steeped in sin.

When we are tempted, we need to stop at the initial stage of entertaining the sin. At that point we need to say, "No! I choose to be holy and righteous."

---

5. Peter was the one who deserved mocking because he fell so short of his recent boasts. In **Luke 22:33** Peter had said, **"Lord, I am ready to go with you to prison and to death."**

6. Then the cock crowed, as Jesus had prophesied. In **Luke 22:61** we read, **"The Lord turned and looked straight at Peter."** How traumatic this confrontation with Jesus must have been for Peter! The penalty for Peter's sin was to face, not Jesus' anger, but the heartbreak in His eyes.

7. Peter denied Christ not only from fear of bodily harm, but also from his unwillingness to endure the same disgrace and humiliation that Jesus suffered.

When we are tempted to deny our faith in Jesus because we fear rejection and disapproval from others, let us remember the heartbreak in Jesus' eyes. Let us stand firm in our convictions, be willing to bear humiliation, and desire only God's approval.

8. At this point, Peter may have already remembered the words of Jesus: **"And when you have turned back, strengthen your brothers" Luke 22:32b**. It is as if Jesus said, "I know your heart, Peter, you will deny Me. But you will repent and weep bitter tears. The result will be that you will be able to strengthen your brothers because of your mistakes."

9. Peter was quick to repent. He turned back to Jesus and received His forgiveness. Later, when Peter returned to strengthen the other believers, he realized what Jesus had done for him.

10. When we fail Jesus, how quick are we to repent? Do we remember that Jesus bore our sin on the cross, and that God casts our sins into the depths of the sea (**Micah 7:19**)?

Do we allow ourselves to immediately turn back and come into His presence? We must! Jesus chose to be humiliated and to withhold His awesome power, so that we could come into the fullness of intimate relationship with Him.

V. Discussion of the Assigned Article

TIME PERMITTING, ASK ONE PARTICIPANT TO FACILITATE A BRIEF DISCUSSION, POSING QUESTIONS TO DRAW OUT COMMENTS ABOUT THIS ARTICLE. ENCOURAGE THE DISCUSSION LEADER AND PARTICIPANTS TO FOCUS ON PORTIONS OF THE ARTICLE THAT ARE RELATED TO THE MAIN PRINCIPLE.

VI. "Miniature Messengers"

READ ALOUD TO THE CLASS THIS CHAPTER FROM MAX LUCADO'S BOOK *NO WONDER THEY CALL HIM THE SAVIOR*.

VII. Next Week's Assignment

A. REVIEW NEXT WEEK'S ASSIGNMENT ON THE COURSE OUTLINE.

B. REVIEW THE MAIN PRINCIPLE FOR NEXT WEEK'S LESSON.

C. THE FACILITATOR WILL FACILITATE THE SCRIPTURE DISCUSSION. REMIND THE CLASS THAT NEXT WEEK YOU WILL ASK SOMEONE TO LEAD THE BOOK OR ARTICLE ASSIGNMENT. SO, ALL SHOULD BE READY TO LEAD THESE DISCUSSIONS.

VIII. Closing Prayer

END THE LESSON BY PRAYING A CLOSING PRAYER, UNLESS THE LORD INDICATES THAT SOMEONE SHOULD RECEIVE MINISTRY. BE SENSITIVE TO THE HOLY SPIRIT'S GUIDANCE REGARDING HOW TO PRAY. YOU MIGHT WANT TO PRAY WITH THE MAIN PRINCIPLE IN MIND. A SAMPLE PRAYER FOLLOWS:

Thank You, Lord, for enduring scorn and humiliation for us. Forgive us for the times we have failed You and denied You. Enable us to walk in the fear of the Lord, desiring only Your approval and not the approval of others. Strengthen us so that in the future we can be willing to endure humiliation for Your sake. Lead each of us into the fullness of relationship with You that Your suffering made possible. In Jesus' precious name, Amen.

IN HIS PRESENCE

LESSON 8

OUR CHOICE—STAGES THREE AND FOUR

MAIN PRINCIPLE

*We must choose to avoid pride and hardness of heart
and keep our hearts pliable towards the Lord.
We need to choose to let go of our sinful attitudes and
actions when God reveals them to us. As we
truly repent of our sins and turn to Jesus,
we will receive the help and forgiveness we need.*

WWW.ZOEMINISTRIES.ORG

LESSON 8

Our Choices—Stages Three and Four

I. Let's Get Started!

A. WELCOME THE CLASS AND ENCOURAGE PARTICIPANTS TO BRIEFLY SHARE WHAT GOD HAS DONE IN THEIR LIVES DURING THE PAST WEEK.

B. OPEN WITH PRAYER.

C. WORSHIP THE LORD.

D. HAVE SOMEONE READ THE MAIN PRINCIPLE FOR THIS LESSON.

II. Supporting Principles From the Book

ASK ONE PARTICIPANT TO FACILITATE A BRIEF DISCUSSION, ASKING QUESTIONS TO DRAW OUT COMMENTS ABOUT THE ASSIGNED READING. ENCOURAGE THE DISCUSSION LEADER AND PARTICIPANTS TO FOCUS ON PORTIONS OF THE BOOK THAT ARE RELATED TO THE MAIN PRINCIPLE.

III. Discussion of Article "Is God Opposing the Church?"

ASK ONE PARTICIPANT TO FACILITATE A BRIEF DISCUSSION, POSING QUESTIONS TO DRAW OUT

Lesson 8 — Our Choices—Stages Three and Four

COMMENTS ABOUT THIS ARTICLE. ENCOURAGE THE DISCUSSION LEADER AND PARTICIPANTS TO FOCUS ON PORTIONS OF THE ARTICLE THAT ARE RELATED TO THE MAIN PRINCIPLE.

IV. Supporting Principles From Scripture—Matthew 27:1–26
Mark 15:1–15
Luke 22:66–23:25
John 18:28–19:1

A. Review

Stage One: In anguish Jesus chose to obey the Father.
Sweating drops of blood, Jesus suffered spiritually, physically and emotionally.

Stage Two: Jesus endured humiliation.
He was blindfolded, mocked repeatedly, spit upon and struck in the face.

B. **The Sanhedrin had Jesus bound**—Matthew 27:1–2; Mark 15:1; John 18:28

1. The Sanhedrin gathered in the early morning. Legally, they were not supposed to hold a session at night, so at daybreak a special meeting was held for all members to decide how to eliminate Jesus (**Matthew 27:1**).

2. The Jews had no official power to enforce the death sentence. Such a sentence had to be passed by the Roman governor and carried out by the Roman

authorities. It was for this reason that the Jews brought Jesus before Pilate.

3. **Verse 2 reads, "They bound Him, led him away and handed him over to Pilate, the governor."**

WE ARE NOW IN STAGE THREE—THEY BOUND JESUS AND TOOK HIM TO PILATE.
Jesus was bound like a common criminal.

4. The term *bound* is translated from the Greek word *deo* (deh´-o), which means to bind, to throw into chains.[1]

   The Living Bible reads, **"Then they sent him in chains to Pilate, the Roman governor."**

   Jesus, already exhausted and battered, blindfolded and spat upon, was then chained.

5. Jesus' behavior did not warrant this type of treatment! He had never laid a hand on anyone to harm him, and He had not resisted arrest.

6. They bound Him as if He were the worst kind of criminal, not fully realizing that He had willingly submitted to them. He had demonstrated His power to some of them in **John 18:6**; they were unable to hurt Him without His consent.

Jesus allowed Himself to be bound so that
we might be free from bondage.

---

7. It was the priest's pride and hardness of heart that motivated him to have Jesus further humiliated by being bound.

When we sin and pridefully refuse to repent, we, in effect, bind Jesus. We tie His hands from working freely in our lives.

C. The death of Judas—Matthew 27:3–10

1. **"When Judas, who had betrayed him, saw that Jesus was condemned, he was seized with remorse…" Matthew 27:3.**

   a. Judas had assumed that he would be at Jesus' side when Jesus would presumably use God's power to overthrow the oppressive Roman government.

   Do we sometimes presume we know what God should do and then get mad at Him for not doing it? This sin of presumption comes from pride and is a sin to which we are susceptible.

   b. But when Judas saw that Jesus would not overthrow the Romans, but chose death instead, he regretted betraying Jesus.

   Judas' heart attitude at this point becomes clearer when we read this verse from *The Amplified Bible*. **"When Judas, His betrayer, saw that [Jesus] was condemned, [Judas was afflicted in mind and troubled for his former folly; and] with remorse [with little more than a selfish dread of the consequences] he brought back the thirty pieces of silver** to the chief priests and the elders" **Matthew 27:3**.

    c. To be **"seized with remorse"** is translated from the Greek word *metamellomai* (met-am-el´-lom-ahee), which means "to regret; to have deep remorse at the consequence of sin rather than a deep regret at the cause of it. It is never used of genuine repentance to God."[2]

If Judas had truly repented, the Greek word *metanoeo* (met-an-o-eh´-o) would have been used, since it means "to repent; to change one's mind for the better, heartily to amend with abhorrence of one's past sins."[3]

2. When Judas said, **"I have sinned"** (**Matthew 27:4**), he regretted his decision to betray Christ, but he did not truly repent.

///

Many people say, "I have sinned." That is easy to say. They are not forgiven, though, because they do not renounce the sin and go to God with a change of heart.

///

3. Judas threw the money into the temple (**Matthew 27:5**). More exactly, he threw the coins into the sanctuary of the temple. *Vincent's Word Studies of the New Testament* says, "He cast the pieces over the barrier of the enclosure which surrounded the sanctuary, or temple proper, and within which only the priests were allowed...."[4]

It is interesting that Judas would throw the money into the Holy Place. He probably wanted to undo some of the evil he had done.

Lesson 8 — Our Choices—Stages Three and Four

4. The chief priests said that it was unlawful to accept this blood money and they instead put it into the temple treasury. Yet, they were guilty of condemning to death the Son of God! It is amazing how we can be deluded and justify sin.

5. Judas hanged himself at the Field of Blood, the potter's field. Subsequently, this was where foreigners were buried. This is fitting because Judas became like a foreigner to Jesus' other disciples. Judas was not a brother in Christ; he went where he belonged—to hell (**Acts 1:18, 19, 25**).

6. Satan had entered Judas (**John 13:27**) and the outcome was death. No matter how you look at it, without repentance and a change of heart, the result is death. Satan, who had tempted Judas into presumption, then pushed him to despair.

D. "Well…Almost"

READ ALOUD TO THE CLASS THIS CHAPTER FROM MAX LUCADO'S *NO WONDER THEY CALL HIM THE SAVIOR*.

///
Today, when He is silent, He can be saying the same thing to us, "Examine yourself."
///

E. **Jesus before Pilate—Matthew 27:11–14; Mark 15:2–5; Luke 23:1–23; John 18:29–38**

1. Earlier the charge against Jesus was blasphemy—speaking contemptuously about God (**Matthew 26:65**). However, this was not the charge on which they brought Jesus before Pilate.

The charges against Jesus that they brought before Pilate are spelled out in **Luke 23:2: "We have found this man subverting our nation. He opposes payment of taxes to Caesar and claims to be Christ, a king."** They presented political reasons for Pilate to condemn Jesus, not religious reasons. Pilate would have been able to dismiss the charges against Jesus if they were simply related to the Jewish religion.

2. When Jesus stood before the governor, Pilate asked Him, **"Are you the king of the Jews,"** Jesus replied, **"Yes, it is as you say" Matthew 27:11.**

    In **John 18:36–37** Jesus further elaborated, revealing that He is a king and that His kingdom is not of this world.

3. The chief priests and the elders slandered and wrongly accused Jesus (**Matthew 27:12**).

    Do we wrongly accuse God of things for which He is not guilty—such as blaming Him for a bad circumstance in which we find ourselves—yet we ourselves are at fault?

4. Jesus' answer to their charges was neither no nor yes. Pilate believed Jesus was innocent and he urged Jesus to clear Himself. This would have given Pilate the justification he needed for Jesus' release (**Matthew 27:12–14**).

5. From this point on, Jesus refused to speak. Jesus' silence fulfilled the words of **Isaiah 53:7. "He was oppressed and afflicted, yet he did not open his mouth; he was led like a lamb to the slaughter,**

and as a sheep before her shearers is silent, so he did not open his mouth."

6. In Jesus' silence, it was as if He was saying, "Examine yourself—not me. See who is truly sinning!"

7. Pilate did not want to condemn Jesus. So, he sent Jesus to Herod, hoping to avoid the consequences of making a judgment against this holy man (**Luke 23:7**).

8. When Jesus wouldn't answer Herod's questions, Herod and his soldiers ridiculed and mocked Jesus (**Luke 23:9–11**).

Silence can be very threatening! There are times when silence is more eloquent than words, *for silence can convey things that words can never say!*

9. Both Jews (the chief priests) and Gentiles (Pilate) were responsible for Jesus' mistreatment and death.

F. Jesus was sentenced to death—Matthew 27:15–26; Mark 15:6–15

1. The crowd went to Pilate, seeking the release of a prisoner, as the Roman governor always allowed during the Feast of Passover (**Mark 15:6**). Pilate, seeing this opportunity as a way to avoid condemning Jesus, offered to release Him. He asked the crowd, **"Which one do you want me to release to you: Barabbas, or Jesus who is called Christ?"** Matthew 27:17. Barabbas' name means "son of the father",[5] which is ironic because Jesus actually is the Son of God the Father.

2. Barabbas was a **"notorious prisoner"** (**Matthew 27:16**) and **"had taken part in a rebellion"** (**John 18:40**). The choice seemed clear to Pilate, but the chief priest and Jewish officials persuaded the crowds to ask for the release of Barabbas.

3. Think of the crowd and their choice. The choice was releasing Barabbas or releasing Jesus—a criminal involved in a murderous plot or Jesus, a sinless man—darkness versus light. They chose darkness.

4. Pilate's wife confirmed Pilate's desire to release Jesus when she sent word to him of a dream she had regarding Jesus' innocence (**Matthew 27:19**).

5. Pilate's greatest sin was compromising what he knew to be true and right, for the sake of status (pride) and personal gain. Pilate knew Christ was innocent, and declared this fact on several occasions (**Luke 23:4, 14, 20**).

6. The crowd unknowingly prophesied when they said, **"Let his blood be on us and on our children!"** (**Matthew 27:25**). They said this as if it were of no consequence. In actuality, our being covered by Jesus' blood is the only way we can have eternal life and come into God's presence.

G. **Jesus was flogged and delivered to be crucified—Matthew 27:26**

WE ARE NOW IN STAGE FOUR—JESUS WAS FLOGGED.

1. We should not diminish the fact that Jesus underwent flogging, or scourging. The following quote from *The Fire Bible—ESV* elaborates on this practice:

   > The Roman flogging consisted of the victim being stripped and stretched against a pillar or bent over a low post with the hands tied. The instrument of torture was a short wooden handle that had several strips of leather attached to it. Bits of iron or bone were interwoven into the pieces of leather. Two men usually whipped the victim, one lashing the victim from one side, one from the other side. This resulted in the flesh being cut so severely that veins, arteries and sometimes even inner organs were exposed. Sometimes victims died during the flogging.[6]

2. This type of treatment "was designed to get confessions and secrets from its victims, but what could they get from an innocent, sinless one...?"[7]

3. *Dake's Annotated Reference Bible* provides more information:

   > Flogging was permitted by the law up to 40 stripes (Dt 25:3). Jews reduced this to 39 stripes (2 Cor. 11: 23–25). If the scourge used on Jesus had 12 thongs and He was hit even 39 times this would make 468 stripes. If some struck in the same place and cut deeper each time one can see how His body, because of the intense hatred [in] back of each blow, was marred more than any other man's (Isa. 52:14).[8]

So we see that Jesus' flogging fulfilled the prophecy in **Isaiah 52:14**, which says, **"Just as there were many who were appalled at him—his appearance was so disfigured beyond that of any man and his form marred beyond human likeness...."**

H. Conclusion

1. The following people in today's reading all walked in pride and hardness of heart toward God, and refused to repent of their sins:

    a. *Judas* chose to remain in his sin and did not fully repent. This choice prevented him from receiving Jesus' love and forgiveness.

    b. The chief priests' envy prevented them from receiving anything from God (**Matthew 27:18**). They pridefully chose to remain in their sin of envy, which kept God bound from working in their lives.

    c. *Pilate* chose to placate the crowd and did not risk his position as governor—even though he knew Jesus was innocent and he could have saved Him. Pilate refused to admit this sin, declaring his innocence.

2. *Consider the difference between Peter and these other men.* Peter's sin was just as bad—he denied Jesus when He needed him most. Yet, Peter's heart was soft enough toward God to feel a conviction of sin, and he responded with true repentance. This released God's power into Peter's life to bring about the needed changes in his heart.

Today, people walk in pride and hardness of heart similar to that of Judas, the chief priests and Pilate. We must choose to keep our hearts pliable towards the Lord. Like Peter, we need to truly repent of our sinful attitudes and actions when God reveals them to us, and turn to Jesus for help and forgiveness.

V. Discussion of the Assigned Article "The Marvelous Benefits of Repentance!"

TIME PERMITTING, ASK ONE PARTICIPANT TO FACILITATE A BRIEF DISCUSSION, POSING QUESTIONS TO DRAW OUT COMMENTS ABOUT THIS ARTICLE. ENCOURAGE THE DISCUSSION LEADER AND PARTICIPANTS TO FOCUS ON PORTIONS OF THE ARTICLE THAT ARE RELATED TO THE MAIN PRINCIPLE.

VI. "Come Home"

READ ALOUD TO THE CLASS THIS CHAPTER FROM MAX LUCADO'S *NO WONDER THEY CALL HIM THE SAVIOR*.

VII. Next Week's Assignment

A. REVIEW NEXT WEEK'S ASSIGNMENT ON THE COURSE OUTLINE.

B. REVIEW THE MAIN PRINCIPLE FOR NEXT WEEK'S LESSON.

C. THE FACILITATOR WILL FACILITATE THE SCRIPTURE DISCUSSION. REMIND THE CLASS THAT NEXT WEEK YOU WILL ASK SOMEONE TO LEAD THE BOOK OR ARTICLE ASSIGNMENT. SO, ALL SHOULD BE READY TO LEAD THESE DISCUSSIONS.

VIII. Closing Prayer

END THE LESSON BY PRAYING A CLOSING PRAYER, UNLESS THE LORD INDICATES THAT SOMEONE SHOULD RECEIVE MINISTRY. BE SENSITIVE TO THE HOLY SPIRIT'S GUIDANCE REGARDING HOW TO PRAY. YOU MIGHT WANT TO PRAY WITH THE MAIN PRINCIPLE IN MIND. A SAMPLE PRAYER FOLLOWS:

Thank You, Lord, that You desire to work in our hearts and free us from bondage to sin. Show us if we are walking in pride or hardness of heart. Help us be willing to change and to surrender our sinful attitudes and actions when You reveal them to us. Help us to *truly* repent—until the fruit of righteousness is brought forth in our lives. We pray in Jesus' name, Amen.

IN HIS PRESENCE

LESSON 9

THE ROBE, THE CROWN AND THE CROSS—STAGES FIVE AND SIX

MAIN PRINCIPLE

Just as Jesus was stripped of His clothes and His dignity, so we need to be stripped of any idols we have. As God reveals them, we must completely tear down all idols in our lives. Then we can enter into God's presence with hearts free of idolatry.

LESSON 9

The Robe, the Crown and the Cross— Stages Five and Six

I. Let's Get Started!

A. WELCOME THE CLASS AND ENCOURAGE PARTICIPANTS TO BRIEFLY SHARE WHAT GOD HAS DONE IN THEIR LIVES DURING THE PAST WEEK.

B. OPEN WITH PRAYER.

C. WORSHIP THE LORD.

D. HAVE SOMEONE READ THE MAIN PRINCIPLE FOR THIS LESSON.

II. Supporting Principles From the Book

ASK ONE PARTICIPANT TO FACILITATE A BRIEF DISCUSSION, ASKING QUESTIONS TO DRAW OUT COMMENTS ABOUT THE ASSIGNED READING. ENCOURAGE THE DISCUSSION LEADER AND PARTICIPANTS TO FOCUS ON PORTIONS OF THE BOOK THAT ARE RELATED TO THE MAIN PRINCIPLE.

III. Supporting Principles From Scripture—
Matthew 27:27–32
Mark 15:16–21

A. Review

Stage One:
In anguish Jesus chose to obey the Father.
Sweating drops of blood, Jesus suffered spiritually, physically and emotionally.

Stage Two:
Jesus endured humiliation.
He was blindfolded, mocked repeatedly, spit upon and struck in the face.

Stage Three:
They bound Jesus and took Him to Pilate.
Pilate questioned Him.

Stage Four:
Jesus was flogged.
Pilate handed Him over to be crucified.

B. Matthew 27:27

1. Even though Pilate pronounced Jesus innocent, he handed Jesus over to his Roman soldiers to be crucified.

2. The soldiers took Jesus into the palace, probably while the cross was being prepared for His crucifixion.

3. Jesus was taken into the Praetorium, a section of the governor's palace. There He was surrounded by an entire company of Roman soldiers.

WE ARE NOW IN STAGE FIVE—THEY STRIPPED JESUS OF HIS CLOTHES AND DIGNITY.

In scorn, they dressed Him in a robe and a crown of thorns and struck Him.

C. "And they stripped off His clothes and put a scarlet robe (garment of dignity and office worn by Roman officers of rank) upon Him" Matthew 27:28 (AMP).

1. How humiliating to be stripped and to stand naked before all those soldiers!

2. Then the soldiers put a red robe on Jesus. According to *Eerdmans Bible Dictionary*, "garments of scarlet were considered a contribution toward beauty…and were particularly worn by aristocracy…and royalty."[1] A person wearing a scarlet robe would be deemed worthy of an honored position. Perhaps this robe was the cast-off cloak of some high Roman officer. They put it over the body of Jesus to mock Him, not knowing that He holds the most honored position.

3. Think of the fresh pain Jesus experienced as His clothes were pulled off His bloody, mutilated back!

D. "And, weaving a crown of thorns, they put it on His head and put a reed (staff) in His right hand. And kneeling before Him, they made sport of Him, saying, Hail (greetings, good health to You, long life to You), King of the Jews! And they spat on Him, and took the reed (staff) and struck Him on the head" Matthew 27:29–30 (AMP).

Lesson 9 — The Robe, The Crown and the Cross—Stages Five and Six

1. Mocking Jesus as an imposter king, they placed the "crown" of thorns on His head. The soldiers designed it to be painful for Jesus, viciously pressing the thorns down into His forehead and skull.

2. Placing a counterfeit staff in Jesus' right hand, imitating a coronation, was another way they mocked him. They ridiculed Him with the insincere salutation of **"Hail, King of the Jews!"** Their sarcasm becomes more evident as we realize that *Hail* can mean "long life to you."

3. Instead of kissing Jesus, which was a sign of honor towards a king, they spit in Jesus' face.

4. They repeatedly struck Jesus on the head with the staff, a symbol of kingship.

5. The actions of these soldiers were cruel, but they bore Him no personal malice. To them, Jesus was just another man being prepared for the cross and crucifixion—something that was not new to them. This was mean-spirited horseplay on the part of the soldiers, but their behavior was far less sinful than the malicious deeds of the accusing Jewish leaders.

6. Consider what had happened to Jesus up to this point—the denial by His disciples, the hateful actions of the Jewish leaders, Pilate's cowardly behavior, the flogging, and now this additional pain and humiliation.

   Isaiah 53:3a was definitely fulfilled that day: **"He was despised and rejected by men, a man of sorrows, and familiar with suffering."**

7. Jesus underwent all this misery and shame so that He might purchase for us everlasting life, joy and glory.

WE ARE NOW IN STAGE SIX— JESUS WAS FORCED TO CARRY A CROSS AS THEY LED HIM OUT TO BE CRUCIFIED.

E. "And when they finished making sport of Him, they stripped Him of the robe and put His own garments on Him and led Him away to be crucified. As they were marching forth, they came upon a man of Cyrene named Simon; this man they forced to carry the cross of Jesus" Matthew 27:31–32 (**AMP**).

   1. After the soldiers had mocked and abused Christ, they took the robe from Him. No mention is made of their removing the crown of thorns, so we can assume that Jesus still endured it.

   2. They led Jesus away to be crucified as a lamb would be led to the altar for sacrifice. READ **ISAIAH 53:7A**: **"He was oppressed and afflicted, yet he did not open his mouth; he was led like a lamb to the slaughter."**

   3. By now the cross was prepared and, like a common criminal, Jesus had to carry it to the place of execution.

   4. According to **John 19:17**, Jesus began by carrying His own cross. He was like Isaac, who carried the wood for the burnt offering (**Genesis 22:6**).

      Forcing a criminal to carry his own cross was intended to cause more pain and to further shame him.

5. Picture Jesus: battered, bruised, scorned, rejected, spit upon, His head bleeding, His back flogged so that the flesh was exposed. And now, on top of all this, He was forced to carry a heavy, rough cross. Soldiers were all around Him, perhaps kicking and mocking and spitting on Him. He staggered through the streets of Jerusalem, forced to take the longest, most painful route for all to see.

6. But under the weight of the cross, Jesus' strength failed and He could not continue. At this point, Simon of Cyrene was forced to carry it; a man from what is now Libya carried the cross for Jesus.

F. Conclusion

1. Jesus was stripped of His dignity and anything that might lend Him security. *We* must be willing to be stripped of the idols in *our* lives.

2. Jesus allowed Himself to be humiliated. Are we willing to tear down all the self-bolstering idols we cling to as God points them out to us?

If we seek to enter into God's presence and to stand before His throne, we need to come with a heart free of idols—free of self and our rebellious, independent ways.

---

3. At this point in the course, we may be feeling picked on. We may be weary of looking at our sinful nature. Under a heavy conviction from the Holy Spirit at this point, it may seem too hard. However, God wants us to go through this process.

Jesus endured so much for us. Can't we endure dying to self and crucifying our fleshly desires? This may be uncomfortable, but look at it from God's perspective. He would be justified in saying to us sarcastically, "Oh, so you have a twinge of discomfort...Yet, look at what my Son endured for you!"

4. God is jealous; He wants every part of us. If we are serious about going into His presence, we need to let go of our idols in light of what Jesus did for us.

IV. "Pao, Senor?"

READ ALOUD TO THE CLASS THIS CHAPTER FROM MAX LUCADO'S *NO WONDER THEY CALL HIM THE SAVIOR*.

As we express our gratitude toward Him by stripping ourselves of idols, how we please our beloved Lord.

V. Discussion of the Assigned Articles

TIME PERMITTING, ASK ONE PARTICIPANT TO FACILITATE A BRIEF DISCUSSION, POSING QUESTIONS TO DRAW OUT COMMENTS ABOUT THESE ARTICLES. ENCOURAGE THE DISCUSSION LEADER AND PARTICIPANTS TO FOCUS ON PORTIONS OF THE ARTICLES THAT ARE RELATED TO THE MAIN PRINCIPLE.

VI. Next Week's Assignment

A. REVIEW NEXT WEEK'S ASSIGNMENT ON THE COURSE OUTLINE.

B. REVIEW THE MAIN PRINCIPLE FOR NEXT WEEK'S LESSON.

C. THE FACILITATOR WILL FACILITATE THE SCRIPTURE DISCUSSION. REMIND THE CLASS THAT NEXT WEEK YOU WILL ASK SOMEONE TO LEAD THE BOOK OR ARTICLE ASSIGNMENT. SO, *ALL* SHOULD BE READY TO LEAD THESE DISCUSSIONS.

VII. Closing Prayer

END THE LESSON BY PRAYING A CLOSING PRAYER, UNLESS THE LORD INDICATES THAT SOMEONE SHOULD RECEIVE MINISTRY. BE SENSITIVE TO THE HOLY SPIRIT'S GUIDANCE REGARDING HOW TO PRAY. YOU MIGHT WANT TO PRAY WITH THE MAIN PRINCIPLE IN MIND. A SAMPLE PRAYER FOLLOWS:

Thank You, Jesus, for what You endured for our sake. Lord, show each of us the idols in our life. Help us to completely tear down those idols in obedience to You. Help us to be completely dependent on You and to forsake our independent ways. Renew and increase our love for You so that we will make those sacrifices from hearts of love and gratitude. Give a revelation of Your love for each of us. We pray in Jesus' name, Amen.

IN HIS PRESENCE

LESSON 10

CARRYING THE CROSS—
STAGES SEVEN AND EIGHT

MAIN PRINCIPLE

*Jesus suffered greatly when He was crucified.
We need to respond to Jesus' suffering at His crucifixion
by choosing to take up our cross and follow Him.
We must not be like the Pharisees, who were more
concerned with religion than following Jesus.*

LESSON 10

Carrying the Cross—
Stages Seven and Eight

I. Let's Get Started!

    A. WELCOME THE CLASS AND ENCOURAGE PARTICIPANTS TO BRIEFLY SHARE WHAT GOD HAS DONE IN THEIR LIVES DURING THE PAST WEEK.

    B. OPEN WITH PRAYER.

    C. WORSHIP THE LORD.

    D. HAVE SOMEONE READ THE MAIN PRINCIPLE FOR THIS LESSON.

II. Supporting Principles From the Book

ASK ONE PARTICIPANT TO FACILITATE A BRIEF DISCUSSION, ASKING QUESTIONS TO DRAW OUT COMMENTS ABOUT THE ASSIGNED READING. ENCOURAGE THE DISCUSSION LEADER AND PARTICIPANTS TO FOCUS ON PORTIONS OF THE BOOK THAT ARE RELATED TO THE MAIN PRINCIPLE.

III. Supporting Principles from Scripture—
Matthew 27:32–44
Mark 8:34–38; 15:21–32
Luke 23:26–43
John 19:17–27

A. Review

Stage One:
In anguish Jesus chose to obey the Father.
Sweating drops of blood, Jesus suffered spiritually, physically and emotionally.

Stage Two:
Jesus endured humiliation.
He was blindfolded, mocked repeatedly, spit upon and struck in the face.

Stage Three:
They bound Jesus and took Him to Pilate.
Pilate questioned Him.

Stage Four:
Jesus was flogged.
Pilate handed Him over to be crucified.

Stage Five:
They stripped Jesus of His clothes and dignity.
In scorn, they dressed Him in a robe and crown of thorns and struck Him.

Stage Six:
Jesus was forced to carry a cross as they led Him out to be crucified.

B. Matthew 27:32–34

1. Christ was led away, carrying His cross to Golgotha (**John 19:17**). However, under its weight, Jesus' strength failed and He could carry it no longer. It is no wonder, considering what Jesus had endured up to that point.

2. It was customary for criminals condemned to death to carry the beam of a cross to the place of crucifixion.

3. When Jesus' strength failed, Simon of Cyrene was pressed into service. Carrying a criminal's cross would have been a reproach; no one would do it except by compulsion (**verse 32**). And yet, this was surely the greatest honor any man ever had.

Are we ready to respond in such a way for Jesus—
willing to accept reproach for Jesus' sake?

---

4. Simon was from Cyrene, which is in Africa. Why was he in Jerusalem? **Mark 15:21** states that he was passing by on his way from the country to Jerusalem. Perhaps he was going to Jerusalem for the Feast of the Passover.

    a. He may have been completely unaware of what was occurring and understandably reluctant when forced to carry a beam for a criminal. How unpleasant it would have been to carry the heavy, blood-stained cross.

    b. Did something happen to him as he followed Jesus, carrying the cross through Jerusalem's winding streets? Could there have been something about Jesus that drew him? Once they reached Golgotha, did he have an encounter with the living Lord? Scripture indicates that something happened to Simon that changed the direction of his life.

- In **Mark 15:21** made reference to Simon as the father of Alexander and Rufus. This description was meant to identify him. He must have been a man and/or father of importance.

- His son, Rufus, may have been the Rufus to whom Paul referred as **"chosen in the Lord" Romans 16:13**.

- In **Acts 11:20** there is mention of men from Cyrene who were instrumental in the first mission to the Gentiles. Could Simon have been one of them?

5. Simon was *forced* to take up Jesus' cross and follow Him to Golgotha. Are we *willing* to take up our cross and follow Jesus?

6. **How would you define carrying one's cross?**

HAVE PARTICIPANTS TURN TO THIS PASSAGE:
Mark 8:34–35 says, "If anyone would come after me, he must deny himself and take up his cross and follow me. For whoever wants to save his life will lose it, but whoever loses his life for me and for the gospel will save it."

Carrying one's cross involves denying yourself and doing what Jesus would do. It means crucifying the desires of our flesh and choosing to walk in holiness.

Jesus forgave His executioners (**Luke 23:34**). When people do or say hurtful things to us are we willing to forgive just as Jesus did? Are we willing to endure scorn for being a disciple of Jesus? Are we willing to carry the gospel where the Lord leads?

7. Jesus was offered wine mixed with gall (**Matthew 27:34**).

    a. Gall was a plant-derived substance with a very bitter taste. *Unger's Bible Dictionary* comments: "The Jews were in the habit of giving the criminal a stupefying drink before nailing him to the cross, probably with the purpose of deadening pain."[1] This correlates with the myrrh mentioned in **Mark 15:23**.

    b. After tasting the wine, Jesus refused it because it was drugged with gall. He chose to taste death at its bitterest and to go to God fully aware (**Matthew 27:34**).

Sometimes we are called to go through pain in order to get where God wants us spiritually. We may need to forego those things that serve as distractions or painkillers, so we can focus on what God desires to do in our hearts.

Lesson 10 — Carrying the Cross—Stages Seven and Eight

WE ARE NOW IN STAGE SEVEN—JESUS WAS CRUCIFIED.

C. Matthew 27:35

1. *The Fire Bible—ESV* gives the following description of the crucifixion:

   The cross beam is placed on the ground and Jesus is laid on it. His arms are stretched along the beams and a heavy, square, wrought-iron nail is driven through his hand (or wrist) and deep into the wood. Next, Christ is lifted up by means of ropes or ladders, and the cross beam is tied or nailed to an upright beam with a support for the body fastened onto it. His feet were then extended and a larger piece of iron is driven through them.[2]

2. It was the third hour, or nine in the morning, when they crucified Jesus. Remember, this was the same time that the temple priests were preparing the Passover lambs for sacrifice.[3]

3. The Roman soldiers assigned to a crucifixion detail stripped the criminals naked and were allowed to keep their clothing. Only the basest of criminals were crucified. Jesus, the Son of the living God, was stripped naked and nailed to the cross. How humiliating!

4. **John 19:23** mentions how the soldiers divided Jesus' garments. His undergarment, or tunic, was without seam, woven from the top in one piece. This is the exact description of the linen undergarment worn by the High Priest, whose function was to be the liaison between God and man.

"When John mentions the seamless tunic of Jesus it is not just a description of the kind of clothes that Jesus wore; it is something which tells us that Jesus is the perfect priest, opening the perfect way for all men to the presence of God."[4]

5. Perhaps Mary, Jesus' mother, had made this tunic. Had she pondered the connection between Jesus and the priestly robe? As she watched the soldiers gamble for it, how did she feel?

D. **Matthew 27:36**

1. **Verse 36** says that the soldiers sat there and kept watch over Jesus—not mentioning the other criminals. The soldiers now knew that this was no ordinary prisoner; they knew this was no ordinary man. They knew that some people had called Jesus the Son of God (**verse 54**).

2. They kept a careful watch over Jesus because their jobs and perhaps their lives would be in jeopardy if anyone rescued Him.

E. **"Close to the Cross—But Far from Christ"**

READ ALOUD TO THE CLASS THIS CHAPTER FROM MAX LUCADO'S BOOK *NO WONDER THEY CALL HIM THE SAVIOR.*

F. **Matthew 27:37–38**

1. The charge against each crucified criminal was posted on the cross over his head. Above Jesus' head was a notice reading, **"This is Jesus, the King of the Jews."**

2. **John 19:19–22** tells us that Pilate had that notice prepared and placed on Jesus' cross. Recall how the angry crowd pressured Pilate to crucify Jesus. He knew that the Pharisees had incited that crowd. There is no doubt that Pilate put this inscription on the cross of Jesus to irritate and annoy the Jews. They had just said that they had no king but Caesar; they had absolutely refused to have Jesus as their king. The Jewish leaders repeatedly asked him to remove it, and Pilate refused. He said, **"What I have written, I have written" John 19:22.**

3. So the sign proclaimed for all to see Jesus' true title instead of the charge against Him. The inscription was written in Hebrew, Greek and Latin. It was written for all people to read, just as Jesus came to earth for every tongue, tribe and nation!

4. Two robbers were crucified with Jesus—one on His right and one on His left. What a contrast—the Son of God and two thieves! This was not a coincidence. Jesus came to save *all* people.

Are we willing to die to self and show love to others when we are in pain, physical or emotional?

G. READ **JOHN 19:25–27.**

In a time of great suffering and sorrow, we see Jesus continuing to show limitless love, especially toward those who were dear to Him.

H. "Leaving is Loving"

READ ALOUD TO THE CLASS THIS CHAPTER FROM MAX LUCADO'S BOOK *NO WONDER THEY CALL HIM THE SAVIOR.*

WE ARE NOW IN STAGE EIGHT—THEY HURLED INSULTS AT JESUS.

I. Matthew 27:39–40

1. At this point, Jesus was a horrific sight. He was exhausted, blood-streaked, covered with wounds, and exposed to the view of His enemies. He had experienced pain in His entire body for hours. He suffered from fatigue in His arms, great waves of cramps in His muscles, and intense thirst. More agony came with a crushing pain deep in His chest as fluid began to compress His heart.

2. **Matthew 27:39** says, **"Those who passed by hurled insults at him, shaking their heads."** Now, in addition to all this physical pain, insults and ridicule were thrown at Him. Could this deep, helpless sense of rejection be the most excruciating pain thus far?

3. **Psalm 22:7** prophesied exactly what occurred in **verse 39: "All who see me mock me; they hurl insults, shaking their heads."**

4. Passers-by misquoted what Jesus had said after He cleared the money-changers from the temple (**John 2:19**). The Jews had asked Him by what authority He had done this. Jesus answered, **"Destroy this temple, and I will raise it again in three days."** With this, Jesus predicted His death and resurrection. There would be no resurrection if He

Lesson 10 — Carrying the Cross—Stages Seven and Eight

now heeded their mocking taunts to save Himself and come down from the cross (**verse 40**).

J. **Matthew 27:41–44**

1. These were probably the same people who demanded that Pilate enforce the charges they brought against Jesus. They were enjoying their victory, ridding themselves of this man who threatened their position of authority. How depraved—mocking a dying man!

    a. Why were these priests and others visiting Jesus on the cross? This was the time of Passover. Shouldn't they have been in the temple? They claimed their religion was the only true one, and they were the only representatives of God.

    b. These religious leaders undoubtedly knew that Jesus had claimed to be the Messiah. They said that they would believe in Him if He came down from the cross (**verse 42**).

    They sealed their fate when they said this; they missed receiving eternal life with God. Jesus said that everyone who believed in the Son of Man would have eternal life (**John 3:15**).

    c. What was spoken in **verse 43** was prophesied in **Psalm 22:8**: **"He trusts in the Lord; let the Lord rescue him. Let him deliver Him, since he delights in him."**

2. In **Luke 23:36** the soldiers also mocked Jesus, offering Him vinegar to drink. They knew it would

not satisfy His thirst, which was now a torment due to Jesus' extreme blood loss.

3. **Matthew 27:44** says that the robbers who were crucified with Jesus also insulted Him, but **Luke 23:39–43** differentiates between the two criminals. One hurled insults at Jesus; the other defended Him.

   a. Both men were criminals, but their hearts were different. One had a soft heart and the other's heart had hardened. One criminal was heading to paradise and spiritual life with Jesus; the other was heading toward hell and spiritual death.

   b. The robber who defended Jesus understood the fear of the Lord. He acknowledged his sin and asked for mercy and forgiveness. He confessed Jesus as Lord.

   c. How encouraging for Christ, that even in His most agonizing moment He was given a lost soul to enter paradise with Him. And it was also a wonderful reminder of what He had come to do—to save souls. What a victory for Christ and what a defeat for the enemy!

K. **"Words That Wound"**

   READ ALOUD TO THE CLASS THIS CHAPTER FROM MAX LUCADO'S BOOK *NO WONDER THEY CALL HIM THE SAVIOR.*

Lesson 10 — Carrying the Cross—Stages Seven and Eight

L. Note to Facilitators

IT MAY BE HELPFUL TO SHARE THE FOLLOWING WITH THE CLASS.

During this course, we examine all that Jesus endured for us so that we can be free from sin and guilt. Yet, when we realize that we continue to sin despite God's love and provision for us, we may begin to experience a sense of hopelessness or a feeling of condemnation. We need to be able to differentiate between conviction of sin by the Holy Spirit and condemnation from the enemy.

When the Holy Spirit convicts us, He brings our attention to a specific sin. He usually shines His light on only one sin at a time. The conviction brings with it a promise of forgiveness and restored fellowship with God. Once we agree with God about our sin and lay it down at the foot of the cross, we are free to go on in our relationship with the Lord.

On the other hand, Satan often brings vague condemnation. **"The accuser of our brethren"** (**Revelation 12:10 KJV**) may try to overwhelm us by pointing out all the situations in our life that are not right. His accusations evoke shame and fear of being in God's presence. The condemnation of Satan drives us away from God.

Let us heed only the convicting work of the Holy Spirit, who brings life and serves to bring us back into God's presence.

IV. Discussion of the Assigned Articles

TIME PERMITTING, ASK ONE PARTICIPANT TO FACILITATE A BRIEF DISCUSSION, POSING QUESTIONS TO DRAW OUT COMMENTS ABOUT THESE ARTICLES. ENCOURAGE THE DISCUSSION LEADER AND PARTICIPANTS TO FOCUS ON PORTIONS OF THE ARTICLES THAT ARE RELATED TO THE MAIN PRINCIPLE.

V. Next Week's Assignment

A. REVIEW NEXT WEEK'S ASSIGNMENT ON THE COURSE OUTLINE.

B. REVIEW THE MAIN PRINCIPLE FOR NEXT WEEK'S LESSON.

C. THE FACILITATOR WILL FACILITATE THE SCRIPTURE DISCUSSION. REMIND THE CLASS THAT NEXT WEEK YOU WILL ASK SOMEONE TO LEAD THE BOOK OR ARTICLE ASSIGNMENT. SO, ALL SHOULD BE READY TO LEAD THESE DISCUSSIONS.

VI. Closing Prayer

END THE LESSON BY PRAYING A CLOSING PRAYER, UNLESS THE LORD INDICATES THAT SOMEONE SHOULD RECEIVE MINISTRY. BE SENSITIVE TO THE HOLY SPIRIT'S GUIDANCE REGARDING HOW TO PRAY. YOU MIGHT WANT TO PRAY WITH THE MAIN PRINCIPLE IN MIND. A SAMPLE PRAYER FOLLOWS:

Help us to take up our cross and follow Jesus. Enable each of us to crucify the desires of our flesh and choose to walk in holiness. Help us to be like Jesus and forgive people even when they treat us harshly. Help us endure reproach for Jesus' sake. Help each of us not to be like the Pharisees, who were more concerned with religion than with truly following Jesus. We pray in Jesus' name, Amen.

IN HIS PRESENCE

LESSON 11

DEPARTURE FROM HIS PRESENCE—STAGES NINE AND TEN

MAIN PRINCIPLE

We need to understand the significance of Jesus' final words, "It is finished." It was a shout of victory! Jesus won access to God for us because He was willing to take on our sin and be separated from the Father. As we go into God's presence, we go in humility and gratitude, but also in victory.

WWW.ZOEMINISTRIES.ORG

LESSON 11

Departure From His Presence— Stages Nine and Ten

I. Let's Get Started!

A. WELCOME THE CLASS AND ENCOURAGE PARTICIPANTS TO BRIEFLY SHARE WHAT GOD HAS DONE IN THEIR LIVES DURING THE PAST WEEK.

B. OPEN WITH PRAYER.

C. WORSHIP THE LORD.

D. HAVE SOMEONE READ THE MAIN PRINCIPLE FOR THIS LESSON.

II. Supporting Principles From the Book

ASK ONE PARTICIPANT TO FACILITATE A BRIEF DISCUSSION, ASKING QUESTIONS TO DRAW OUT COMMENTS ABOUT THE ASSIGNED READING. ENCOURAGE THE DISCUSSION LEADER AND PARTICIPANTS TO FOCUS ON PORTIONS OF THE BOOK THAT ARE RELATED TO THE MAIN PRINCIPLE.

III. Discussion of the Article "Wrestling With God"

ASK ONE PARTICIPANT TO FACILITATE A BRIEF DISCUSSION, POSING QUESTIONS TO DRAW OUT COMMENTS ABOUT THIS ARTICLE. ENCOURAGE THE DISCUSSION LEADER AND PARTICIPANTS TO FOCUS ON PORTIONS OF THE ARTICLE THAT ARE RELATED TO THE MAIN PRINCIPLE.

IV. Supporting Principles From Scripture—
Matthew 27:45–50
John 19:28–30
Psalm 139:7–8
Jeremiah 23:24
Deuteronomy 30:11–20

A. Review

Stage One:
In anguish Jesus chose to obey the Father.

Stage Two:
Jesus endured humiliation.

Stage Three:
They bound Jesus and took Him to Pilate.

Stage Four:
Jesus was flogged.

Stage Five:
They stripped Jesus of His clothes and dignity.

Stage Six:
Jesus was forced to carry a cross as they led Him out to be crucified.

Stage Seven:
Jesus was crucified.

Stage Eight:
They hurled insults at Jesus.

B. "Final Words, Final Acts"

READ ALOUD TO THE CLASS THIS CHAPTER FROM MAX LUCADO'S BOOK *NO WONDER THEY CALL HIM THE SAVIOR.*

C. Matthew 27:45
"From the sixth hour until the ninth hour darkness came over all the land."

1. Jesus was crucified at the third hour, around 9 a.m., according to **Mark 15:25**. Matthew tells us that the darkness lasted from the sixth hour until the ninth hour, meaning from noon until 3:00 p.m.[1] This is an odd time of day for darkness to overcome the land. How ominous and frightening that must have been!

2. Was God allowing creation to reflect in a material way the spiritual darkness of this time? The term *darkness* often represents the concept of sin. During those dark hours on the cross Jesus took on the sin of all mankind. What physical agony He endured as He "bore our sins in his body" (1 Peter 2:24). It was as if the creation reflected the distress of its Creator.

Lesson 11 — Departure From His Presence—Stages Nine and Ten

D. Matthew 27:46

"About the ninth hour Jesus cried out in a loud voice, 'Eloi, Eloi, lama sabachthani?' (e-lo´-ee, e-lo´-ee, la´-mah sa-bak´-tha-ni)—which means, 'My God, my God, why have you forsaken me?'"

WE ARE NOW IN STAGE NINE—"MY GOD, WHY HAVE YOU FORSAKEN ME?"

1. As Jesus bore the sin of the world, **"God made Him who had no sin to be sin for us"** according to **2 Corinthians 5:21**. Jesus endured the full impact and weight of mankind's sin. Because the holiness of the Father required that He turn away from His Son, Jesus experienced a separation from the Father that He had never known, since the beginning of time.

2. When Jesus could no longer bear the separation from His Father, He cried out, **"My God, my God, why have you forsaken me?"** This was a direct quote from **Psalm 22:1a**.

3. At this point Jesus' sorrow, grief and torment were at their worst. Could this be what Jesus dreaded when He prayed in the Garden of Gethsemane, asking the Father to take this "cup" away from Him? The physical agony of carrying our sins was horrible enough, but even worse was the spiritual separation from God.

4. He suffered a double death—spiritual and physical—so that we would never have to

E. Matthew 27:47–49 and John 19:28–30

1. Some people standing nearby thought Jesus was calling to Elijah (**Matthew 27:47**). In **verse 49, others said, "Now leave him alone. Let's see if Elijah comes to save him."** A footnote from *The NIV Study Bible* states: "The bystanders mistook the first words of Jesus' cry ('Eloi, Eloi') to be a cry for Elijah. It was commonly believed that Elijah would come in times of critical need to protect the innocent and rescue the righteous...."[2]

2. **John 19:28** says, **"Knowing that all was now completed, and so that Scripture would be fulfilled, Jesus said, 'I am thirsty.'"** This verse implies that Jesus was fully conscious and was aware of fulfilling the prophecy of **Psalm 63:1: "O God, you are my God, earnestly I seek you; my soul thirsts for you, my body longs for you, in a dry and weary land where there is no water."**

3. Someone offered Jesus a sponge filled with wine vinegar. Wine vinegar was the equivalent of cheap wine, possibly diluted with water, and was the drink of ordinary people.[3] Jesus did drink from this sponge (**John 19:30**).

4. The vinegar-soaked sponge was placed on the end of a stalk from a hyssop plant (**John 19:29**). Perhaps John included this detail in his account to point to Jesus as the true Passover Lamb since hyssop was used in the Passover ceremony (**Exodus 12:22**). It was the blood of the Passover lamb that saved the

people of God; it was the blood of Jesus that would save the whole world from sin.

5. It is a paradox that the One who said, **"Whoever drinks of the water I give him will never thirst"** (John 4:14) died with extreme thirst.

F. **"I Thirst"**

READ ALOUD TO THE CLASS THIS CHAPTER FROM MAX LUCADO'S BOOK *NO WONDER THEY CALL HIM THE SAVIOR.*

G. READ THE FOLLOWING EXCERPT FROM H.A. MAXWELL WHYTE'S BOOK, *THE POWER OF THE BLOOD:*

> Imagine, if you can, the scene at Calvary. No artist has ever pictured the Calvary scene as it really was. It would be too repulsive to paint on any canvas. It is doubtful that the Romans left Jesus even the courtesy of a loincloth. He became as the first Adam in the garden, that He might cover His nakedness with His own precious Blood—not even a linen cloth to spoil the type. In turn, we may cover our nakedness with his precious Blood—a perfect atonement or covering indeed! We cannot even offer a convenient loincloth or fig leaf to hide our sins; we must divest ourselves of everything and appear destitute of all covering in His presence. Then He will give us His own blessed robe of righteousness after we have accepted the cleansing of His precious Blood. A glorious truth indeed!
>
> The crown of thorns was then put upon His head, not gently but roughly; many thorns (maybe a

dozen or more), one-and-a-half inches long, jabbed into His scalp, producing such serious wounds that trickles of Blood spurted out and ran into His hair and beard, matting both in dark red. The spikes were driven into the palms of His hands, and His Blood coursed down His arms and sides. (Later the spear was thrust into His side and His Blood spilled out and ran down the sides of the cross onto the ground beneath.) Spikes were also driven through His feet and more Blood ran down the sides of the cross on behalf of the sins of the whole world.

His bones were out of joint (Ps. 22). His face was dreadful to look upon. There was no beauty in Him that we should desire Him (Is. 53:2). God gave His best, His Son, His perfect sacrifice—and even in death, there was no blemish in Him, for He was already dead when the soldiers arrived to break His legs; therefore, not a bone of Him was broken. Those who looked on Him saw only Blood. It was a spectacle of Blood. His hair and beard were soaked in His own Blood. His back was lacerated from the thirty-nine stripes and was covered with His own Blood. Even the cross was covered with Blood, and the very earth was soaked. Every type of the atonement was fulfilled in Christ. It was the Blood, Blood, Blood.[4]

WE ARE NOW IN STAGE TEN—JESUS CRIED, "IT IS FINISHED!"

H. Matthew 27:50
"And when Jesus had cried out again in a loud voice, he gave up his spirit."

Lesson 11 — Departure From His Presence—Stages Nine and Ten

1. Three of the gospels tell us that Jesus died with a great shout upon His lips. Only in John 19:30 do we hear Jesus cry out, "It is finished." This statement referred to many things: the payment of the penalty for our sins, the fulfillment of Scriptures about the suffering of the Messiah, the defeat of Satan, the establishment of personal access to God, the cancellation of sin's power, to name a few.[5] But most of all, it communicated the victory Jesus had won!

2. Jesus did not say, "I am finished," instead He said, "It is finished." Jesus did not go out with a whimper; He went out with a great shout of victory!

3. In **Luke 23:46** Jesus bowed His head, said, **"Father, into your hands I commit my spirit,"** and then breathed His last.

    a. Jesus gave up His spirit for us, so that we could receive the Holy Spirit.

    b. Jesus was permeated with sin for us. We need to give up sin in order to be permeated with the Holy Spirit.

I. **Psalm 139:7–8**
   "Where can I go from your Spirit? Where can I flee from your presence? If I go up to the heavens, you are there; if I make my bed in the depths, you are there."

   1. God assures us that there is no place we can go where His Spirit won't be with us. There is no place we can go that is denied access to God's presence.

2. While on the cross, Jesus suffered separation from the Father's presence, to make it possible for us to gain personal access to God.

J. **Jeremiah 23:24**
"'Can anyone hide in secret places so that I cannot see him?' declares the Lord. 'Do not I fill heaven and earth?' declares the Lord."

We shouldn't try to hide our sin from God; He sees all. He sees to the depths of our sin. God sees and will expose those places in us that are not in accordance with His will.

K. **Deuteronomy 30:11–20—Choose life or death!**

1. God has made it possible for us—and given us the choice—to obey His written Word and His personal word to us. He commands us to love Him and walk in His ways. We need to be humble, recognizing that His ways are better than our ways. We must listen to His voice and obey, for the Lord is our life.

2. We have no life in and of ourselves. Just as Jesus became total sin for us at His crucifixion, He is total life for us. For without Him permeating every area of our lives, we have only sin and death.

A total exchange must occur—our lives for His life. This happens step-by-step, just as Jesus walked step-by-step to the cross and death. As we choose life and put away sin, the fullness of God, who is life, will rest upon us.

L. Conclusion

It was a step-by-step process by which Jesus took on our sin, until finally He was no longer in God's presence. The situation with us is completely the reverse—we are born into sin and begin our lives totally separated from God. But as we accept Jesus' atoning work on the cross for our sin, we receive His Spirit and have access to God's presence. As we allow God's Spirit to expose areas of darkness, and we repent, the Holy Spirit will establish Jesus' nature in us. Then we can come into God's presence not only in humility and gratitude, but also in Jesus' victory.

V. Discussion of the Assigned Articles

TIME PERMITTING, ASK ONE PARTICIPANT TO FACILITATE A BRIEF DISCUSSION, POSING QUESTIONS TO DRAW OUT COMMENTS ABOUT THESE ARTICLES. ENCOURAGE THE DISCUSSION LEADER AND PARTICIPANTS TO FOCUS ON PORTIONS OF THE ARTICLES THAT ARE RELATED TO THE MAIN PRINCIPLE.

VI. Next Week's Assignment

A. REVIEW NEXT WEEK'S ASSIGNMENT ON THE COURSE OUTLINE.

B. REVIEW THE MAIN PRINCIPLE FOR NEXT WEEK'S LESSON.

C. THE FACILITATOR WILL FACILITATE THE SCRIPTURE DISCUSSION. REMIND THE

CLASS THAT NEXT WEEK YOU WILL ASK SOMEONE TO LEAD THE BOOK OR ARTICLE ASSIGNMENT. SO, *ALL* SHOULD BE READY TO LEAD THESE DISCUSSIONS.

VII. Closing Prayer

END THE LESSON BY PRAYING A CLOSING PRAYER, UNLESS THE LORD INDICATES THAT SOMEONE SHOULD RECEIVE MINISTRY. BE SENSITIVE TO THE HOLY SPIRIT'S GUIDANCE REGARDING HOW TO PRAY. YOU MIGHT WANT TO PRAY WITH THE MAIN PRINCIPLE IN MIND. A SAMPLE PRAYER FOLLOWS:

Thank You, Lord, for taking our sin on Yourself. Help us exchange our strength and lives for Your life. Completely envelope and permeate every dimension of our lives. Help us live in complete surrender to Your will and in perfect trust of Your power. Help us repent when the Holy Spirit exposes any areas of darkness in us. Deepen our union and fellowship with You, Jesus, so that Your presence in us makes us holy and victorious. We pray in Jesus' name, Amen.

IN HIS PRESENCE

LESSON 12

PAST THE VEIL AND INTO HIS PRESENCE

MAIN PRINCIPLE

We can now enter the Holy of Holies, the presence of God the Father. We do this only through the shed blood of Jesus, which cleanses us from sin. We can go into God's presence with confidence through Jesus, our new and living way.

WWW.ZOEMINISTRIES.ORG

LESSON 12

Past the Veil and Into His Presence

I. **Let's Get Started!**

    A. WELCOME THE CLASS AND ENCOURAGE PARTICIPANTS TO BRIEFLY SHARE WHAT GOD HAS DONE IN THEIR LIVES DURING THE PAST WEEK.

    B. OPEN WITH PRAYER.

    C. WORSHIP THE LORD.

    D. HAVE SOMEONE READ THE MAIN PRINCIPLE FOR THIS LESSON.

II. **Discussion of the Article "Seven Women Shall Lay Hold of One Man"**

    ASK ONE PARTICIPANT TO FACILITATE A BRIEF DISCUSSION, POSING QUESTIONS TO DRAW OUT COMMENTS ABOUT THIS ARTICLE. ENCOURAGE THE DISCUSSION LEADER AND PARTICIPANTS TO FOCUS ON PORTIONS OF THE ARTICLE THAT ARE RELATED TO THE MAIN PRINCIPLE.

III. **Supporting Principles From the Book**

    ASK ONE PARTICIPANT TO FACILITATE A BRIEF DISCUSSION, ASKING QUESTIONS TO DRAW OUT COMMENTS ABOUT THE ASSIGNED READING.

Lesson 12 — Past the Veil and Into His Presence

ENCOURAGE THE DISCUSSION LEADER AND PARTICIPANTS TO FOCUS ON PORTIONS OF THE BOOK THAT ARE RELATED TO THE MAIN PRINCIPLE.

IV. Supporting Principles From Scripture—
Exodus 26:31–33
Matthew 27:50–54
Hebrews 9:3, 7–14
Hebrews 10:19–22

A. Review

Stage One:
In anguish Jesus chose to obey the Father.

Stage Two:
Jesus endured humiliation.

Stage Three:
They bound Jesus and took Him to Pilate.

Stage Four:
Jesus was flogged.

Stage Five:
They stripped Jesus of His clothes and dignity.

Stage Six:
Jesus was forced to carry a cross as they led Him out to be crucified.

Stage Seven:
Jesus was crucified.

Stage Eight:
They hurled insults at Jesus.

Stage Nine:
"My God, why have you forsaken me?"

Stage Ten:
Jesus cried, "It is finished!"

B. **"Creative Compassion"**

READ ALOUD TO THE CLASS THIS CHAPTER FROM MAX LUCADO'S *NO WONDER THEY CALL HIM THE SAVIOR.*

C. Background—In **Exodus 26:31–33**, God directed Moses to put a curtain between the Holy Place and the Most Holy Place. The Ark of the Covenant was kept in the Most Holy Place and was the location of God's very Presence. The Lord required a separation between His Presence and things that were not absolutely holy.

D. **Matthew 27:50–54**
HAVE SOMEONE READ THIS PASSAGE ALOUD.

1. At the time of Jesus' death, three momentous events occurred:

    a. The curtain of the temple was torn in half from top to bottom.

    b. There was a strong earthquake that split rocks.

    c. Many holy people were raised from the dead.

2. There was profound significance in the fact that the temple curtain was torn.

   a. *The Fire Bible* comments: "The tearing of the 'curtain of the temple'…signified that a way was now open into the presence of God. The curtain separating the Holy Place from the Most Holy Place represented sinful humanity's separation from a holy God. Access was restricted to all except the high priest—and then only under strict conditions at the appointed time. Jesus filled the role of the ultimate high priest…with full access to God the Father. Through his death, Jesus made the ultimate sacrifice for our sin, tore back the curtain into the Most Holy Place (i.e., God's presence) and opened permanent access to God for all who surrender their lives to him…."[1]

   b. Jesus' death occurred at the time of the evening sacrifice, and priests would be officiating at the temple. They probably were eye-witnesses as the temple curtain split in half. Can you imagine their shock?

   c. The fact that this occurred from top to bottom signified that God is the One who ripped the thick curtain. It was not torn from the bottom by humans. God was inviting everyone into His presence thereafter—not only the Old Testament high priest.

   d. Although the temple had been a place reserved solely for Jewish worship, now, through Christ, Jews and Gentiles could have access to God.

e. The mysteries were unveiled; we all, with unveiled faces, can behold the glory and goodness of the Lord.

///

God's rending of the curtain was forceful, even violent. We, too, must forcefully deal with our hearts' barriers that keep us from entering into God's presence.

///

3. At the moment Jesus died, a powerful earthquake occurred, actually splitting rocks. Possible explanations of the significance of this earthquake follow:

   a. The death of Christ was a supernaturally powerful event, with repercussions impacting even creation.

   b. Did this begin the fulfillment of the prophecy in **Haggai 2:7: "I will shake all nations, and the desired of all nations will come, and will fill this house with glory"?** Was God foreshadowing what He would do through Jesus' sacrifice?

   c. The earthquake demonstrated that Christ's sacrifice dealt the fatal blow to Satan's kingdom. God's victory was also demonstrated another time when an earthquake released Paul from his bonds in prison (**Acts 16:26**). Remember also the shaking that occurred after the believers prayed in one accord for boldness to preach God's word (**Acts 4:31**).

Lesson 12 — Past the Veil and Into His Presence

    d. When the rocks split, it was as if the hardest and firmest part of the earth gave way to this mighty shock.

//

As we consider Christ's death, our hard and rocky hearts must yield. A hardened heart that will not give way when Jesus Christ's crucifixion is explained is harder than a rock that will not split.

//

4. The opening of the tombs of many holy people pointed to the following:

    a. Matthew Walvoord and J. Dwight Pentacost, in their book *Thy Kingdom Come*, suggest that this event was "a fulfillment of the Feast of the Firstfruits of the harvest mentioned in **Leviticus 23:10–14**. On that occasion, as a token of the coming harvest, the people would bring a handful of grain to the priest. The resurrection of these saints, occurring after Jesus Himself was raised, is a token of the coming harvest when all the saints will be raised."[2]

    b. Jesus' death marked the defeat of death for all of mankind. **Isaiah 25:7–8a reads, "On this mountain he will destroy the shroud that enfolds all peoples, the sheet that covers all nations; he will swallow up death forever."**

//

As believers, we are so fortunate to have the assurance that after we physically die, we will continue to experience eternal life.

//

5. **"When the centurion and those with him who were guarding Jesus saw the earthquake and all that had happened, they were terrified, and exclaimed, 'Surely he was the Son of God!'"** verse 54.

   a. The Roman soldiers had heard the people ridicule Jesus saying, **"Come down from the cross, if you are the Son of God!" verse 40**. Now, after seeing all that happened, they believed Jesus was the Son of God.

   b. They not only believed He was God's Son, but they were terrified at the prospect of God's response! When we walk in the fear of the Lord, we also declare with our lives, "Jesus is the Son of God!"

   c. These were Gentile soldiers. They were not familiar with the Scriptures whose prophecies were being fulfilled, yet they were convinced! Despite all that happened, the Jewish leaders still continued to deny Jesus' deity. It is sad that Jesus' disciples, who knew Jesus was the Son of God, did not publicly confess it at this time.

E. Hebrews 9:3, 7–14; 10:19–22

   1. **Hebrews 9:8** reads, **"The Holy Spirit was showing by this that the way into the Most Holy Place had not yet been disclosed as long as the first tabernacle was still standing."** A footnote in *The NIV Study Bible* explains that the phrase **"as long as the first tabernacle was still standing"** is like saying, "as long as the Mosaic

system with its imperfect priesthood and sacrifice remained in effect."³

2. **"The way into the Most Holy Place"** described in **Hebrews 9:8** is the blood of Jesus. His blood covers us and cleanses us so that we might confidently enter the presence of God the Father (**Hebrew 10:19–20**).

   Jesus alone is the great High Priest and the perfect sacrifice for our sins.

3. Jesus' body is the curtain that was torn to give us access to God the Father (**Hebrews 10:20**).

F. READ ALOUD THE FOLLOWING STORY:

What Was In Jeremy's Egg?
The Lesson of Easter from an Unlikely Child

By Ida Mae Kempel

Jeremy was born with a twisted body and slow mind. At the age of 12 he was still in second grade, seemingly unable to learn. His teacher, Doris Miller, often became exasperated with him. He would squirm in his seat, drool and make grunting noises.

At other times, he spoke clearly and distinctly, as if a spot of light had penetrated the darkness of his brain. Most of the time, however, Jeremy irritated his teacher. One day, she called his parents to come to St. Theresa's for a consultation. As the Forresters sat quietly in the empty classroom, Doris said to them, "Jeremy really belongs in a special school. It isn't fair to him to be with younger children who don't have learning problems.

Why, there is a five-year gap between his age and that of the other students!"

Mrs. Forrester cried softly into a tissue, while her husband spoke. "Miss Miller," he said, "there is no school of that kind nearby. It would be a terrible shock for Jeremy if we had to take him out of this school. We know he really likes it here."

Doris sat for a long time after they left, staring at the snow outside the window. Its coldness seemed to seep into her soul. She wanted to sympathize with the Forresters. After all, their only child had a terminal illness. But it wasn't fair to keep him in her class. She had 18 other youngsters to teach, and Jeremy was a distraction. Furthermore, he would never learn to read and write. Why waste any more time trying?

As she pondered the situation, guilt washed over her. "Oh God," she said aloud, "here I am complaining when my problems are nothing compared to that poor family! Please help me to be more patient with Jeremy!"

From that day on, she tried hard to ignore Jeremy's noises and his blank stares. Then one day, he limped to her desk, dragging his bad leg behind him. "I love you, Miss Miller," he exclaimed, loud enough for the whole class to hear. The other students snickered, and Doris' face turned red. She stammered, "Wh-why that's very nice, Jeremy. N-now please take your seat."

Spring came, and the children talked excitedly about the coming of Easter. Doris told them the story of Jesus, and then to emphasize the idea of new life springing forth, she gave each of the children a large plastic egg.

Lesson 12 — Past the Veil and Into His Presence

"Now," she said to them, "I want you to take this home and bring it back tomorrow with something inside that shows new life. Do you understand?"

"Yes, Miss Miller!" the children responded enthusiastically—all except for Jeremy. He just listened intently; his eyes never left her face. He did not even make his usual noises.

Had he understood what she had said about Jesus' death and resurrection? Did he understand the assignment? Perhaps she should call his parents and explain the project to them. That evening, Doris' kitchen sink stopped up. She called the landlord and waited an hour for him to come by and unclog it. After that, she still had to shop for groceries, iron a blouse and prepare a vocabulary test for the next day. She completely forgot about phoning Jeremy's parents.

The next morning, 19 children came to school, laughing and talking as they placed their eggs in the large wicker basket on Miss Miller's desk. After they completed their math lesson, it was time to open the eggs.

In the first egg, Doris found a flower. "Oh yes, a flower is certainly a sign of new life," she said. "When plants peek through the ground we know that Spring is here." A small girl in the first row waved her arm. "That's my egg, Miss Miller," she called out.

The next egg contained a plastic butterfly, which looked very real. Doris held it up. "We all know that a caterpillar changes and grows into a beautiful butterfly. Yes, that is new life, too." Little Judy smiled proudly and said, "Miss Miller, that one is mine!"

Next, Doris found a rock with moss on it. She explained that moss, too, showed life. Billy spoke up from the back of the classroom, "My Daddy helped me!" he beamed.

Then Doris opened the fourth egg. She gasped. The egg was empty! Surely it must be Jeremy's, she thought, and of course, he did not understand her instructions. If only she had not forgotten to phone his parents! Because she did not want to embarrass him, she quietly set the egg aside and reached for another.

Suddenly Jeremy spoke up. "Miss Miller, aren't you going to talk about my egg?" Flustered, Doris replied, "But Jeremy—your egg is empty!" He looked into her eyes and said softly, "Yes, but Jesus' tomb was empty, too!"

Time stopped. When she could speak again, Doris asked him, "Do you know why the tomb was empty?" "Oh yes!" Jeremy said, "Jesus was killed and put in there. Then His Father raised Him up!"

The recess bell rang. While the children excitedly ran out to the school yard, Doris cried. The cold inside her melted completely away.

Three months later, Jeremy died. Those who paid their respects at the mortuary were surprised to see 19 eggs on top of his casket, all of them empty.[4]

This is a true story. The names have been changed for sake of privacy. This article appeared in Focus on the Family, April, 1988, and is used here by permission of the author. Ida Mae Kempel is a free-lance writer from Alameda, California.

G. Discussion of the Assigned Article

TIME PERMITTING, ASK ONE PARTICIPANT TO FACILITATE A BRIEF DISCUSSION, POSING QUESTIONS TO DRAW OUT COMMENTS ABOUT THIS ARTICLE. ENCOURAGE THE DISCUSSION LEADER AND PARTICIPANTS TO FOCUS ON PORTIONS OF THE ARTICLE THAT ARE RELATED TO THE MAIN PRINCIPLE.

H. Closing

As we conclude this time together, let us once again reflect on one of the most loving Scriptures in all of the Bible.

READ **JOHN 3:16–17** IN *THE AMPLIFIED BIBLE:*

For God so greatly loved and dearly prized the world that He [even] gave up His only begotten (unique) Son, so that whoever believes in (trusts in, clings to, relies on) Him shall not perish (come to destruction, be lost) but have eternal (everlasting) life. For God did not send the Son into the world in order to judge (to reject, to condemn, to pass sentence on) the world, but that the world might find salvation and be made safe and sound through Him.

Do we really acknowledge the depth of the Father's love? Do we fully acknowledge the obedience and love of the Son? Do we truly acknowledge the great sacrifice made on our behalf by both the Father and Son, so we might once again be allowed directly into the presence of God? Let us never lay aside the power of the Cross, Jesus' sacrifice and the power of His resurrection!

V. Share what God has done in our lives during this course.

These past weeks we have looked carefully at Christ's betrayal, trial, crucifixion and death. Hopefully, our first love for Jesus has been renewed—as when we initially realized what He did for us on the cross. During this course, we may have become aware of how specific sins impede our love relationship with God. We've learned about the power of Jesus' blood and how it can cleanse us as we turn to Him in repentance. The Lord may have spoken to us about taking up our cross and following Him in certain areas of life.

How has this course personally impacted your life?

VI. Break Bread Together

This time of breaking bread together is a celebration of what God has done for us. We rejoice in the renewal of our first love for Jesus because of what He did for us on the cross. We are thankful that the offering of Jesus' blood allows us to confidently come into God's presence.

A. A GLASS OF JUICE AND A PLATE OF BREAD MAY BE SET ON A SMALL TABLE IN THE CENTER OF THE ROOM. SAY, "NOW AS WE BREAK BREAD TOGETHER, LET US REMEMBER WHAT JESUS DID FOR US, AND APPROPRIATE ALL THAT HIS DEATH PROVIDES FOR US."

B. HAVE THE HOST OR THE ASSISTANT FACILITATOR READ **1 CORINTHIANS 11:23–29**.

C. THEN EACH BELIEVER MAY PARTAKE OF THE ELEMENTS. THIS CAN BE DONE INDIVIDUALLY OR CORPORATELY, AS THE HOLY SPIRIT LEADS.

VII. Worship the Lord

TIME PERMITTING, END THE CLASS WITH A TIME OF WORSHIP.

VIII. Ending Notes to Facilitators

IF PARTICIPANTS EXPRESS AN INTEREST IN TAKING ANOTHER ZOE TRAINING COURSE, CONTACT A ZOE REPRESENTATIVE. A LIST OF ZOE COURSE DESCRIPTIONS IS IN THE APPENDIX SECTION OF THE STUDY GUIDE.

ENCOURAGE PARTICIPANTS TO READ ABOUT OUR COURSES ON THE WEBSITE AT WWW.ZOEMINISTRIES.ORG/ZOE-COURSES.

ENDNOTES

Scripture quotations used appear from the following versions:
Holy Bible, New International Version, Zondervan Bible Publishers, Grand Rapids, Michigan, 1988.
The Amplified Bible, Zondervan Publishing House, Grand Rapids, Michigan, 1987.
Life Application Bible-The Living Bible, Tyndale House Publishers Inc. and Youth for Christ USA, Wheaton, Illinois,1988.
The Message, Eugene Peterson, NavPress, Colorado Springs, Colorado, 1993.

Scripture quotations are from the New International Version unless otherwise noted.

Lesson 1

1. ['adam] James Strong, LL.D., S.T.D., *Strong's Exhaustive Concordance of the Bible* (Nashville, Tennessee: Thomas Nelson Publishers), #120.

2. [work it] Strong, #5647.

3. [life] H.W.F. Gesenius, *Gesenius' Hebrew-Chaldee Lexicon to the Old Testament* (Grand Rapids, Michigan: Baker Book House, 1979), p. 273, #2416.

4. [fig leaves] H.A. Maxwell Whyte, *The Power of the Blood* (Springdale, Pennsylvania: Whitaker House, 1973), p. 24.

5. [saw] Gesenius, p. 268, #2372.

Lesson 2

1. [phileo] Strong, #5368.

2. [Lord loves] *1,100 Illustrations from the Writings of D.L. Moody* (Grand Rapids, Michigan: Baker Books, 1996).

3. [Lazarus] Finis Jennings Dake, *Dake's Annotated Reference Bible* (Lawrenceville, Georgia: Dake Bible Sales, Inc., 1963), p. 107, column 4, note c.

4. [active love] *1,100 Illustrations from the Writings of D.L. Moody*, p. 179.

5. [three days] William Barclay, *Daily Bible Study-The Gospel of John, Vol. 2*, (Louisville, Kentucky: The John Knox Westminster Press and Scotland: St. Andrews Press, 1975), p. 115-116.

6. [groaned] Strongs, #1690.

7. [troubled] Ibid, #5015.

8. [tears] Author unknown.

9. [fragrance] Paul Lee Tan, Th.D., *The Encyclopedia of 7700 Illustrations* (Rockville, Maryland: Assurance Publishers, 1979), p. 1570, #7142.

10. [Christ / funerals] *1,100 Illustrations from the Writings of D.L. Moody*, p. 1142, #5021.

Lesson 3

1. [colt] *The NIV Study Bible* (Grand Rapids, Michigan: Zondervan Publishing House, 1985), p. 1577, footnote 19:30.

2. [untie] Joseph H. Thayer, D.D., *Thayer's Greek-English Lexicon of the New Testament* (Peabody, Massachusetts: Hendrickson Publishers, 2000), p. 384, #3089.

ENDNOTES

3. [liberty] *Interlinear Greek-English New Testament* (Grand Rapids, Michigan: Baker Book House, 1981), p. 99.

4. [tongue loosed] Dake, p. 43, column 1, note r.

5. [donkey] *The NIV Study Bible*, p. 1471, footnote 21:2.

6. [humble entry] *The Fire Bible—ESV*, (Peabody, Massachusetts: Hendrickson Publishers Marketing, LLC, 2011), p. 1485, footnote 9:9.

7. [Hosanna] Merrill F. Unger, *Unger's Bible Dictionary* (Chicago, Illinois: Moody Press, 1983), p. 500.

8. [Lord] Dake, p. 83, column 4, note p.

9. [The One] Author unknown.

10. [Son in attic] *The Encyclopedia of 7700 Illustrations*, p. 650, #2692.

Lesson 4

1. [population] *The NIV Study Bible* (Grand Rapids, Michigan: Zondervan Publishing House, 1985), p. 1522, footnote 14:2.

2. [first month] Ibid., p. 101, footnote 12:2.

3. [Josephus] Whyte, pp. 60-61.

4. [without defect] Strong, #8549.

5. [blood] Whyte, p. 24.

6. [not raw] Dake, p. 75, column 4, note m.

7. [bitter herbs] *The NIV Study Bible*, p. 101, footnote 12:8.

8. [Passover] Richard Booker, *Jesus in the Feasts of Israel* (South Plainfield, New Jersey: Bridge Publishing, Inc., 1987) pp. 18-27.

Lesson 5

1. [reclining] William Barclay, *Daily Bible Study-The Gospel of Mark*, p. 341.

2. [expensive perfume] Ibid.

3. [what she has done] Ibid., p. 343.

4. [ambition] Ibid., p. 346.

5. [Last Supper] Dake, p. 51, column 4, note h.

6. [Last Supper] *The International Bible Commentary* ((Grand Rapids, Michigan: Zondervan Publishing House, 1986), p. 1149.

7. [Last Supper] Barclay, *Daily Bible Study-The Gospel of Mark*, pp. 348-351.

8. [dips bread] *The NIV Study Bible*, p. 1484, footnote 26:23.

9. [appeal of God's love] Barclay, *Daily Bible Study-The Gospel of Mark*, p. 352.

10. [poured-out life] *The NIV Study Bible*, p. 1523, footnote 14:24

11. [new covenant] Barclay, *Daily Bible Study-The Gospel of Mark*, p. 357.

ENDNOTES

12. [eucharist] Strong, #2169.

Lesson 6

1. [Gethsemane] *The NIV Study Bible*, p. 1485, footnote 26:36.

2. [sorrow] Strong, #3076.

3. [keep watch] Thayer, p. 122, #1127.

4. [cup] *The Fire Bible—ESV*, p. 1586, footnote 26:39.

5. [bloody sweat] Dake, p. 87, column 4, note u.

6. [agony] William Barclay, *Daily Bible Study-The Gospel of Luke*, (Louisville, Kentucky: The John Knox Westminster Press, 1956), p. 283.

7. [a disciple's kiss] Ibid., p. 272.

8. [friend] Thayer, p. 254, #2083.

9. [I am he] Dake, p. 116, column 1, note n.

10. [legion] *The NIV Study Bible*, p. 1485, footnote 26:53.

Lesson 7

1. [extortion] Barclay, *Daily Bible Study-The Gospel of John, Vol. 2*, p. 264.

2. [Annas] Ibid., p. 265.

3. [Sanhedrin] *The NIV Study Bible*, p. 1526, footnote 14:55.

4. [The Mighty One] Strong, #1411.

Lesson 8

1. [bound] Thayer, p. 131, #1210.

2. [remorse] Dake, p. 31, column 4, note k.

3. [repent] Thayer, p. 405, #3340.

4. [money] Marvin R. Vincent, D.D., *Vincent's Word Studies of the New Testament, Vol. 1* (Peabody, Massachusetts: Hendrickson Publishing), p. 143.

5. [Barabbas] Allen C. Myers, Ed., *The Eerdmans Bible Dictionary* (Grand Rapids, Michigan: William B. Eerdmans Publishing Company, 1987), p. 125.

6. [flogging] *The Fire Bible—ESV*, p. 1589, footnote 27:26.

7. [confessions] Dake, p. 32, column 1, note t.

8. [disfigured appearance] Ibid.

Lesson 9

1. [robe] *The Eerdmans Bible Dictionary*, p. 916.

Lesson 10

1. [gall] Unger, p. 388.

2. [crucifixion] *The Fire Bible—ESV*, p. 1589, footnote 27:35.

3. [third hour] Richard Booker, *Jesus in the Feasts of Israel*, pp. 24-25.

4. [Jesus' tunic] Barclay, *Daily Bible Study-The Gospel of John, Vol. 2*, p. 297.

ENDNOTES

Lesson 11

1. [sixth to ninth] *The NIV Study Bible*, p. 1488, footnote 27:45.

2. [calling Elijah] Ibid., p. 1529, footnote 15:35.

3. [wine vinegar] Ibid., p. 1635, footnote 19:29.

4. [the blood] Whyte, pp. 21-22.

5. [It is finished] Dake, p. 121, column 3.

Lesson 12

1. [the torn curtain] *The Fire Bible—ESV,* p. 1590, footnote 27:51.

2. [holy ones raised] Matthew Walvoord and J. Dwight Pentacost, *Thy Kingdom Come* (Grand Rapids, Michigan: Kregel Publications, 1995), p. 236.

3. [first tabernacle] *The NIV Study Bible*, p. 1868, footnote 9:8.

4. [Jeremy's Egg] Ida Mae Kempel, "Jeremy's Egg," *Focus on the Family Magazine*, Colorado Springs, Colorado, 1988.

APPENDIX

Guidelines for a Personal Visit/Phone Call with Discussion Leaders

1. **Before the visit/call:**

    a. Set up a time to visit/call the couple/class member and tell them what the purpose of the visit/call is.

    b. Ask God what He wants to do in this couple/class member so that you will know how to pray for them personally. Ask for His guidance and protection during your time with the leaders.

    c. Look at the class material so that you will be able to answer any questions they have regarding the book, article and Scripture assignments.

2. **During the visit/call:**

    a. Pray that God would bless your time together and that He would bring to mind those things that need to be discussed.

    b. Ask how they are doing. Ask if they are enjoying the course.

    c. Ask if they have read the article **"Guidelines for Leading a Class Discussion."** Ask if they have any questions about this.

    d. Ask them if they have any questions about the information in the book, article or Scripture assignments. Ask if the Holy Spirit has given them any new insights.

e. Ask if they have questions to stimulate discussion.

f. Encourage them to be open to the Holy Spirit's leading as they prepare and lead the class.

g. Pray together and ask the Lord to anoint them for this task.

3. After the visit/call:

a. Pray for God's anointing, guidance and protection of these participants as they serve as discussion leaders.

b. Pray that God would continue to work in their lives.

www.ingramcontent.com/pod-product-compliance
Lightning Source LLC
Chambersburg PA
CBHW051049160426
43193CB00010B/1123